SALTWATER SALMON ANGLING

Bob Mottram

Photos by Karen and Bob Mottram

FRANK AMATO PUBLICATIONS
P.O. Box 82112, Portland, Oregon 97282
(503) 653-8108

Cover: Roger Ross with 25-lb. chinook
— Photo by J. Brower

Copyright 1989 • Bob Mottram • Printed U.S.A.
Book Design: Joyce Herbst • Typesetting: John Francis Michael
ISBN: 0-936608-89-7

Contents

This book is dedicated to
Karen, Cheryl, Dianna and John,
who make everything worthwhile.

Acknowledgements

It is amazing how generous anglers can be with their time and knowledge when a fellow angler seeks their help. Ask a question, and they will take great pains to see that you get a correct answer. If they don't have it, they invariably know of someone who does, or of someone who knows someone who does.

No individual has enough knowledge to write a book like this by himself. These pages contain the accumulated wisdom of numerous fishermen, charterboat skippers, marina operators and fisheries biologists, representing cumulatively hundreds of years of salmon-angling experience. Each of those who contributed to this work is an expert in his own particular geographical or scientific area and, together, they have provided the information a saltwater angler needs to pursue salmon anywhere from Neah Bay, Washington, to Morro Bay, California.

I wish to gratefully acknowledge the contributions of Al Seda, Neah Bay, Wash.; Paul Collins, Clallam Bay, Wash.; John Haller, Pysht, Wash.; Rod Huberty, Union, Wash.; Doug Nalley, Union, Wash.; Dennis McBreen, Port Orchard Wash.; Rick Thomason, Seabeck, Wash.; Russ Orrell, La Conner, Wash.; Vic Nelson, Hansville, Wash.; David Nelson, Edmonds, Wash.; Mike Chamberlain, Lynnwood, Wash.; Dave P. Nelson, Seattle, Wash.; Tom Cromie, Gig Harbor, Wash.; Russ Rogers, Tacoma, Wash.; Dick Geist, Olympia, Wash.; Mike Zittel, Olympia, Wash.; Mark Cedergreen, Westport, Wash.; Chuck Towslee, Westport, Wash.; Neil Kennedy, Ilwaco, Wash.;

Jack Zimmerman, Warrenton, Ore.; Steve Morris, Garibaldi, Ore.; Gary Hettman, Newport, Ore.; Eric Schindler, Charleston, Ore.; Al Mirati, Gold Beach, Ore.;

Jim Englehart, Crescent City, Calif.; Johnny Kinder, Eureka, Calif.; Don La Faunce, Eureka, Calif.; Pete Kalvass, Fort Bragg, Calif.; Al Grover, Menlo Park, Calif.; and Gary Cummings, Bridgeport, Calif.

Special thanks to Pete Hanke of Port Townsend, Wash., and especially to John Willits of Port Angeles, Wash., who went above and beyond the call of duty in providing assistance.

And a very warm and personal thank you to Erling Bergerson of Tacoma, Wash., a wise and able fisherman and good friend, who years ago set me on the path to a lifetime of salmon-angling enjoyment.

Bob Mottram

Preface

⬥ ⬥ ⬥ ⬥ ⬥ ⬥ ⬥ ⬥ ⬥ ⬥ ⬥ ⬥ ⬥ ⬥ ⬥

T HE EGGS HAD BEEN IN THE GRAVEL AT THE bottom of the river for about four months before the tiny fish poked its head out of the rocks for the first time, drawn by dappled sunlight on the water above him.

His mother, a magnificent chinook salmon, had deposited them the previous fall, about the middle of October, after scooping a redd in the gravel with her tail. His father had finned slowly in the clear water beside her, and released a white cloud of milt as she released her precious eggs. The milt had fertilized the eggs on contact.

It was a reproductive miracle – a miracle because both parent fish had had to survive four long years in the hostile North Pacific Ocean, and then find their way back over hundreds of dangerous ocean miles to this Northwest stream. After they spawned they finally died, here in the place where they, too, had been born.

And it was a miracle that this tiny fish, still drawing nourishment from the yolk sac on his belly, had held a winning ticket in nature's lottery of life; the lottery that determines which eggs are fertilized and which find a safe place among the rocks where they will be protected from predators and where the oxygen-rich water of the river can flow freely around them.

This little fish had been especially fortunate. His parents had been among the last to spawn the fall before. That meant that other, later-spawning fish, had not destroyed his mother's nest in an attempt to make their own.

Flooding was minimal that winter, so the eggs were not scoured from their protected place as so many thousands often are. And the mud slide that occurred in January − the one where half a clearcut hillside fell away in winter's rains − occurred a quarter-mile downstream. It killed tens of thousands of fertilized eggs beneath its oxygen-blocking muck, but it missed the part of the river where this fish was developing.

This little fish, its yolk sac finally consumed, began to feed instinctively on microscopic organisms in the stream. But he didn't wander far from where he had emerged. He fed and grew, dodging predators as best he could, for about three months.

Then, about the first of June, he was drawn by an urge. His body was changing, he was starting to smolt, and he knew, without knowing why, that it was time to move downstream.

As he approached the river's mouth, the environment began to change. The water, just a little briny at first, became saltier and saltier. It would mean death for a regular freshwater fish, but this one pushed on. His body was ready for it, and he was able to resist the powerful, dehydrating effects of the salt.

The fish stayed just outside the river's mouth for a long time, in the estuary where freshwater and saltwater mix. Nature was bountiful here, and the tiny organisms on which he fed were everywhere.

Finally, his instincts called him on. He swam out of the estuary and turned north, responding perhaps to a signal from the earth's magnetic field. He knew innately that danger lurked in the darkness of the deeper water, and so he kept to the shallows near the beach, avoiding the lingcod and the rockfish that waited hungrily in the depths. On and on he swam, ever northward, feeding and growing as he went, eventually passing into Canada near the west coast of Vancouver Island. Day by day, the urge to travel grew weaker, and finally it was gone. Here, hundreds of miles from home, he would feed and grow some more, a mid-range predator in an eat-or-be-eaten world.

His diet by now had changed. He was feeding on herring and on candlefish, and was becoming adept at slashing through a school of them, disabling some, then turning and feeding on the injured as the rest fled. He knew that others were hunting him – sea lions and seals and roving pods of killer whales. Sometimes after he had seen or heard the killer whales, days would pass before he would be calm enough to eat again.

All summer long he fed in the rich Canadian waters, gaining skill as a predator, and gaining size and weight. Fall came, and then winter approached. He drifted south, and passed the darker months along the lower reaches of Vancouver Island.

As winter's gloom gave way to longer, brighter days, he drifted north once more, following his food supply. Somehow he avoided the commercial troll fishery that operates off the Vancouver Island coast, and which devastates so many runs of chinook from U. S. streams.

Life rolled on like this, precariously, for two summers more. Then, the summer after that – his fourth in the sea – a yearning began to take hold of him. It was different from anything he had known before. Some of the fish in his year-class already had left these northern waters, a few in that second summer, a few more in the third. This fish hadn't felt that urge. But now his time approached. He started swimming south. He was coming home.

Exactly when the impulse strikes nobody knows. But by July he had reached the Strait of Juan de Fuca, which separates Canada from the United States. He was taking his time, feeding and resting as he came, putting on fat, storing up energy. By late July, the trickle of chinook through the Strait had become a flood, and he was a part of it. He was as lucky as his parents. He managed to avoid the Indian troll boats, the sportfishing fleets, and the predators that remained a constant part of a salmon's life.

The urge to get home called him more and more strongly now. He was eating less and traveling faster, sensing he was near his journey's end. Soon he would be thrashing upstream through the waters of his birth, reveling in their unique delicious scent which had been implanted in his memory so long ago. Then would come an orgy of reproductive delight, draining his body of the last of its energy.

He was swimming more determinedly now, past underwater landmarks he had seen before. Finally he turned into his estuary and moved toward his river, just ahead.

But now something has caught his eye: a flash, and now another, before him in the water. His eye is drawn to the flash like a pin to a magnet, and he glides in its direction.

Ahead, near the surface, he can see a trail of bubbles from the prop of a small boat. Behind the boat and deep – about where he is – comes the flash. It appears to be following the boat. He is closer now, and he can see the source of the light; a silver oblong that is rolling in lazy circles as it moves across his path, picking up the sun's rays even at this depth, and reflecting them as it turns. Behind it is what looks like a squid, moving when the oblong moves, pausing when it pauses, tentacles swaying hypnotically. Something inside the fish stirs. He can't take his eyes off the squid. He's compelled to move closer.

He's almost home. Just a couple of miles to go. The river is calling. But he can't leave the squid. It's not hunger that he feels. Perhaps it's anger – the sight of the squid, moving and pausing, moving and pausing, tentacles swaying, insolent, following the light.

The fish moves into position to attack . . .

* * *

Chapter One

You Can Do It

I T'S A HEART-IN-YOUR-THROAT EXPERIENCE: the excitement you feel when you first see your salmon rod bucking and dancing in its holder on the gunwale of your boat.

All your senses snap to attention. You nearly tingle with anticipation. You slide the rod from its holder, take a few quick turns on the reel, then you lean back on the rod and tie into the fish. As your rod arcs sharply toward the water you realize he's a big one.

The fish erupts, and a shot of adrenaline goes through you as he starts stripping line from your whining reel. The fight is on.

It happens thousands of times a year, all up and down the Pacific coast. And it can happen to you.

There's nothing magical about catching salmon – big, brawny chinook or acrobatic coho that like to dance on their tails. They're creatures of instinct and habit. And, when you appeal to them in the right way, at the right time and in the right place, their impulses take over.

The rest is pure, heart-thumping thrill.

When it comes to salmon, Northwest anglers are luckier than many. They can fish virtually year-round if they're willing to travel a little to do it. In winter, activity is confined pretty much to the protected, inland marine waters of Washington, where anglers pursue immature chinook, known as feeder chinook or blackmouth. These are fish that never go to the ocean, but spend all of the saltwater phase of their lives in Puget Sound, Hood Canal, the San Juan Islands or the Strait of Juan de Fuca.

Don't let the term "immature" fool you, though. A 22-inch-long blackmouth weighs only about 4 pounds. But blackmouth come a lot bigger, sometimes weighing into the high teens, even the low 20s.

Western Washington's resident coho sometimes can be caught in the spring in these same protected waters, and they offer a different kind of fishing altogether. They generally run only 14 to 20 inches, depending on the month, and are fished with flycasting gear or light spinning tackle. On that kind of equipment, they're every bit as exciting as their brawnier brothers.

Some of the finest fishing of all in the Northwest comes with summer. Those soft, sunny days of July and August, dog-days for anglers in so much of the rest of the country, are the time when big, bright chinook surge in from the ocean in waves. They move by the thousands along the Strait of Juan de Fuca and into Puget Sound and the San Juans, up the Columbia River, and into countless other river systems up and down the Pacific coast from Washington to California, feeding voraciously as they go. Behind them come large schools of ocean coho, scouring the currents for food as they make their way back to the gravel beds and hatcheries that spawned them.

This is the time – July through September – when it particularly pays to be flexible, to follow the progress of the runs and to intercept them wherever they happen to be. A good, trailerable boat and a dependable tow vehicle are all you need to turn your summer into the kind of angling experience that fishermen elsewhere dream about. And with a canopied

11

pickup or a comfortable tent, you can do it on a shoestring.

So — let's say you have figured out where the fish are running, you've trailered your boat there and you've launched it. Now how do you go about actually finding the fish?

As a rule, blackmouth and mature chinook are found in relation to bottom structure, just like the bass in a Florida lake. Migrating chinook tend to travel along the beach, often in water no deeper than 70 to 120 feet, and sometimes just a few yards from the water's edge. Blackmouth tend to spend their time around reefs or rockpiles or points of land, sometimes at dropoffs or underwater holes.

They're attracted by the currents, which dip and eddy and swirl around these structures. The currents concentrate the tiny organisms upon which bait fish feed, thereby attracting the bait fish themselves. And where bait fish gather, so do salmon.

Chinook, particularly immature ones, take the course of least resistance. That means you'll find them resting close to the current, but not right in it if they can help it — someplace where they can watch the action and dart out to pick up a morsel without expending too much energy. So pay attention to the tide, particularly if it's strong. If the current is swirling past a point of land, look for blackmouth on the lee side, in the back eddy where floating organisms are going around and around and the bait fish are feeding on them.

If your fathometer tells you there's a ridge or a hump extending across the current, look for blackmouth on the sheltered side of it, not on the side being scoured by the water.

Coho, both mature and immature, are found less often in relation to structure. Mature fish moving up the Strait of Juan de Fuca, for example, often travel several miles from the beach, and it's common for anglers to have to run 5 or 6 miles offshore to find them.

Look for coho in the rips — those places where different tidal currents come together, creating visible breaks or lines in the water. Bait fish often concentrate there, and that's where coho will be feeding.

To find the coho, first find the bait. And to find the bait, follow the birds. Gulls and terns can spot it easily from on

Pump the rod on a big one, and make sure you have a good man on the net.

high, and where gulls are swooping or terns are sitting on the water, dabbling, it's very likely that salmon are present also.

Approach the birds carefully, at low speed, and toss your bait or lure into the water well toward the edge of the feeding flock so you don't disturb it or the fish below.

Mature coho travel fast, and you have to scout for them. But when the first fish hits, you can expect others to follow. Often, a morning's fishing can mean a boatful of anglers prospecting for two or three hours, then 20 minutes of frenzied action as they limit from the same school.

Some anglers will toss a plastic foam cup or a piece of crumpled newspaper into the water at the first strike, then follow that improvised float to keep from getting too far off the school. Remember to pick up the marker after it has served its purpose.

Blackmouth and mature coho and chinook feed upon the same kinds of things, primarily small fish such as herring, anchovies and candlefish. Immature coho feed upon free-floating organisms their first winter in saltwater, often at the same time and place as terns. At this time they're susceptible to certain fly patterns, but they generally won't take bait.

Resident coho switch to a fish diet about April, and can be taken from then on by standard trolling tactics with fresh herring or a variety of small lures.

Although they feed on the same things, coho and chinook respond to different presentations of bait. Chinook like a bait with a lazier roll. When plug-cutting herring for chinook, you should strive for one that revolves about 60 times a minute. If you're trolling for chinook, and nothing seems to be working, the rule of thumb is to troll slower.

Coho like a bait which spins at least twice as fast and which travels more quickly through the water. The rule of thumb with coho is, when all else fails, troll a little faster.

Despite a coho's affinity for speed, all salmon are basically lazy, and you have to keep that in mind to catch them. They're probably not going to go out of their way to take your bait or lure, and that means you have to put it where they are – in the right area, at the right depth – and present it with the kind of action that will trigger their feeding response.

Salmon are not terribly bright, the way a monkey or a dolphin is bright, and the things they get involved in tend to happen automatically. If you present an appropriate bait or lure at an appropriate time and place, with the proper action, you almost certainly will trigger a strike. There's an old saw that's been around about as long as hooks and lines: If you want to catch big fish, use big bait.

A lot of anglers swear by that theory, and biologists say it may be supported by the principle of conservation of energy. A big fish can't afford to burn up a lot of calories chasing a small bait. The energy to be derived from the food must equal or surpass the energy required to catch it. So remember, to entice a large fish, the bait must pass at a speed and at a distance that make it worth pursuing. The larger the bait, the more effort a salmon may be willing to expend to get it.

Many oldtimers who fish nearly year-around for chinook on southern and central Puget Sound do nothing but pull plugs. And many of them pull only large ones — 5 or 6 inches. They say they may get fewer strikes that way, but the fish they catch are bigger.

* * *

Chapter Two

Boats and Motors

FRANKLY, I WAS WORRIED. IT WAS EARLY MAY, and I had pointed my 14-foot runabout down the west side of Blakely Island in the Washington San Juans, heading for Thatcher Pass and then the final sprint to Anacortes.

I'd been fishing with friends for a couple of days, and now family obligations were calling me home. To get there, I had to cross Rosario Strait to the public ramp at Washington Park, where I'd left my trailer and truck. But a brisk southwest wind was blowing, raising whitecaps even there on the protected waters between Blakely and Lopez islands, and it made me uneasy. When I turned the corner into Thatcher Pass my heart sank.

Rosario Strait, open to the wind all the way from the Olympic Peninsula, was a cauldron of seething white. It was more than I wanted to risk in my little boat.

There was a place to go ashore just outside the mouth of the pass – state-owned James Island, with a tiny bay that was somewhat protected and which had a float to tie up to. The island itself was a good place from which to watch the strait.

At first it looked as though I could be stuck there for days. The wind howled without let-up, driving the rain nearly horizontally up the strait. Fortunately, I had a weatherproof backpacker's tent in my boat, and enough food and drink in the ice chest to see me through. But I fretted about what my family might think.

The worrying turned out to be for nothing, though, a couple of hours later. The wind abated briefly, and I cast off quickly and made the 20-minute run to the other side.

Even then the water was lumpy. Hurrying across the open in my relatively flat-bottomed boat was a teeth-rattling ride, and a wet one. The boat ramp at the other side, when it finally came into view, was as welcome as a truckload of popsicles at a grammar school picnic.

I still fish the San Juans every year, and I've crossed Rosario Strait a number of times since that windy day in May. But there was a lesson to be learned from that: Gear up for the kinds of waters you plan to be fishing, and for goodness sake get a boat with a hull that will cut through a chop. Flat-bottomed boats give a ride like a buckboard.

My current boat is just a foot longer than that other, but it's a lot beamier, has more freeboard, and has a canvas top that's a godsend when heavy seas are splashing over the windshield. It also has a modified Deep-V hull that cuts through a chop like a chainsaw through balsa, flattening out the ride and making windy days mild.

Why all this talk about boats? Because salmon fishing is boat fishing. There's no way you can do well consistently from shore. There are places around the Northwest that salmon can be caught from the beach – Fort Worden near Port Townsend is one, and Fox Island near Tacoma is another. But consistent success requires flexibility, and flexibility requires that you fish from a boat.

It doesn't have to be a big one. On central and southern Puget Sound, for example, a lot of fishermen like the 12-foot fiberglass Hi-Laker. It works well for one person in the protected waters around Commencement Bay and Vashon Island, and many fine salmon are taken from it year-around. It doesn't take much to push it, either, and a lot of fishermen use motors of 9.9 to 15 horsepower.

Fourteen-foot aluminum Lunds are seen nearly everywhere in Western Washington. A 9.9 motor will move them nicely with just one person aboard, but they're more commonly powered by 20 or 25 horses.

From there the sky's the limit, in terms of size and sophistication. Glas-Plys, Bayliners, Boston Whalers, Arimas and many others are used in a variety of lengths and configurations. Almost any of them will do.

Some anglers take salmon from rental boats, like this pair in Washington. It would be a good idea to bring your own life vest, so you don't have to rely only on the cushion usually provided with rentals. This beamy, 14-foot fiberglass is adequate on protected waters.

Downrigger fisherman retrieves line after a strike pulled it loose from downrigger. Downriggers provide the most accurate way for a troller to reach a specific depth.

Aluminum runabout works well for anglers. An extension handle on trolling motor permits operator to run boat without bending, important during a long day on the water.

High top on 15-foot Arima allows quick access to stern when a fish hits, and modified "V" hull slices through chop with ease, providing a smooth ride. Built-in fish box and cooler help to conserve space aboard. Arimas are designed and built by a fisherman for fishermen, and this and larger Arima models are becoming more and more popular among West Coast anglers.

Meatliners with stiff, stubby poles troll near Vashon Island in Puget Sound. Rigs include big reels of wire line, and poles are equipped with pulleys instead of guides. Meatliners must mount strong, metal rod holders on their boats.

C-Dory is easy to launch and economical to operate, because of its flat bottom. But same flat bottom will rattle your teeth when planing in choppy seas. This model, with enclosed cabin, is handy in wet climates.

C-Dory with center console provides plenty of fishing space for four anglers. High freeboard is good in rough water, and flat bottom provides excellent stability during fishing, even when anglers cluster along one rail to watch fish come aboard.

A 14-foot Livingston can be an effective salmon boat, with rod holders mounted on gunwales. This one has a mount for a downrigger installed just behind starboard rod holder.

Glas Ply has been popular among Northwesterners for years. A good-quality craft, some models have comfortable, live-aboard features. With this one, a trade-off for some of those comforts is a hard top so high that it's difficult to see over.

This angler has found a way to counter the cold, wet weather that faces Pacific salmon anglers so much of the year.

Here are some points to keep in mind, however. Length overall means little if a lot of it is in front of the windshield, under the covered bow. The space that counts is what's usable for fishing. In a wide-open utility boat, like a Lund or the little Hi-Laker, the entire boat is usable. In a runabout, with a windshield, you're usually confined to the cockpit unless you have a walk-through windshield with an open bow. Some boaters don't like those, though, in heavy seas.

You want fishing room for at least two people. Room for three or more is better. You'll need space for a fish box, if none is built in, for tackle boxes and for stowing a long-handled landing net. You'll want gunwale-mounted rod holders, one per angler, because sooner or later you'll want to set a rod down to pour a cup of coffee.

Holders for storing and transporting rods horizontally along the sides of the boat are very handy. They keep them where you can get at them, and save many a tip from being broken.

If you plan to fish through the winter, consider a boat with some shelter, at least a canvas top. You can feel 15 degrees warmer on a blustery day just by stepping out of the wind. If your cover is canvas, consider the kind that's higher than the top of the windshield. It is much easier to get out of when a rod is dancing in its holder on the stern.

You don't want a cabin or canopy you can't see over, however, when standing in the boat. You'll probably be fishing at least some of the time in crowded waterways, where currents and winds move boats around like traffic on a California freeway, and you've got to have a 360-degree view to keep from colliding. If you don't, one member of the party will have to be a fulltime skipper.

If your main source of power is inboard-outboard, or an outboard of 50 horses or more, you may want a bracket-mounted outboard auxiliary, about 6 horsepower, for trolling. It will double as insurance on bigger waters, getting you home if the big motor conks out.

Consider an auxiliary that will run off the same fuel as the main engine. That means that if the big one's an inboard, or an oil- injected outboard, you should consider a four-cycle auxiliary for which gas and oil aren't mixed. As long as you're carrying an extra 6-gallon tank for the auxiliary anyway, it might as well contain a fuel which is compatible with the large engine and which will extend your range.

No salmon-fishing boat is complete without a fish-finder. One can be mounted in even the smallest utility boat, and should be. It doesn't have to be an expensive, paper graph recorder, although they're certainly efficient, or one of the new LCDs that provide graph-like pictures in color on a liquid crystal display. A simple flasher, if you know how to use it, will get you by. It will tell you not only how far the bottom is beneath your boat, but what kind of bottom it is: muddy, rocky, pinnacled or flat. It will enable you to locate drop-offs and ridges, and will show you schools of bait fish. It will even reveal individual salmon, when properly adjusted.

BOWLINE	CLEATING A LINE

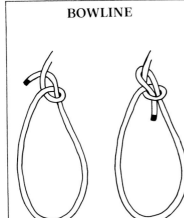

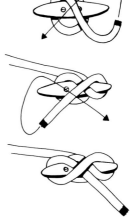

To make a bowline, form an eye in the end of the line far enough away from the rope end to give you the size of loop you require. In the eye the standing part should be underneath.
Lead the free end underneath and through the eye. Then take a turn round the standing part and push the end back through the eye again. Tighten the knot by holding the standing part in one hand, the free end in the other and pulling.

Take a turn round the base of the cleat, then bring the line over the front face of the cleat, below each of the horns in turn in a figure of eight pattern, and back underneath the crossing turn as shown in the bottom drawing. Pull tight. The important thing is that the last turn should lead in the same direction as the standing part.

IMPROVED CLINCH

Insert tag end of line through hook or lure eye and double back, paralleling standing line. Allow at least four inches of tag line for easy handling. Wrap tag end around standing line a minimum of five times.

Insert tag end through loop between first wrap and hook eye. Pull through and insert through large loop. Pinch tag end against standing line with your fingers.

Pull standing line and lure in opposite directions, seating and locking the wraps into neat tight spirals. Be careful that one wrap does not overlap another. Trim tag end tight to knot.

ARBOR KNOT

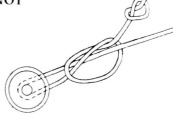

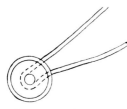

Pass line over and around reel arbor (spool).

Tie a single overhand knot around the line.
Tie a second overhand knot in tag end.

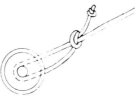

Moisten and snug down against spool arbor.

PALOMAR KNOT

Easier to tie right, and consistently the strongest knot known to hold terminal tackle.

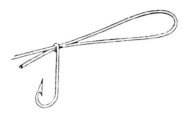

Double about four inches of line and pass loop through eye.

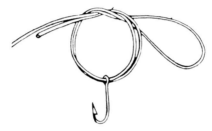

Let hook hang loose and tie overhand knot in doubled line. Avoid twisting the lines and don't tighten knot.

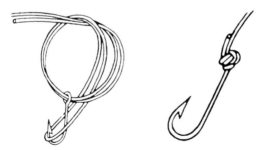

Pull loop of line far enough to pass it over hook, swivel or lure. Make sure loop passes completely over this attachment.

Pull both tag end and standing line to tighten. Clip about 1/8-inch from knot.

Don't opt for a flasher that's built for freshwater, though, despite the fact it may be less costly. You want a model that's calibrated to 60 fathoms, or 360 feet. Anything less will be unsatisfactory.

Mounting your fish-finder's transducer outside the boat will give it the greatest sensitivity. Mounting it inside the hull, if it's properly done, can be satisfactory.

Every boat should have a compass. You may never plot a course with yours, but it's a great help in finding the proper shore in a fog.

Radios are a luxury, but can add to the pleasure, productivity and safety of your trip. VHF, which means very high frequency, is the standard marine radio. With it, anglers can talk boat-to-boat and also ship-to-shore by way of the marine telephone operator, who can put your call through to home. With VHF you also can monitor U. S. and Canadian weather channels.

Many small-boat operators in the Northwest use Citizens' Band radios, and they are perfectly adequate in most circumstances. They're less costly than VHF, and some marine models even have weather channels – something that's lacking in most CBs.

The most common use for CBs among anglers is to share fishing information, and a radio tuned to the local channel can help you to be more productive. Radios sometimes are used for requesting fuel at resorts and marinas where the office is a long way from the water's edge, and are of obvious value if you're drifting with a disabled engine.

Fishermen's CB channels vary from area to area with no apparent pattern. You would communicate on Channel 16 at Neah Bay, for example, Channel 6 at Sekiu, Channel 21 at Port Angeles, Channel 3 on Hood Canal, Channel 10 in the San Juans and Channel 11 around Tacoma.

Ask what the customary channel is where you are fishing.

* * *

Chapter Three

Mooching

————————————————————

HE SAYS IT WAS THE GLOVES THAT DID IT: heavy, woolen gloves with the fingertips missing, the kind that make a wintertime angler look something like one of his own peasant ancestors.

His gloves weren't missing their tips because he was poor, though. They'd been made that way, to permit knot-tying and sensitive thumbing of a reel with a big fish on. And they'd cost plenty – more than eleven bucks for this particular pair.

That's what made it so aggravating. He had one nice salmon in the box already, and was bringing another to the side of the boat, a big chinook. The one on the hook weighed probably 18 or 20 pounds. It came up to the side and the angler turned, his rod in his left hand, and reached for the net with his right. For a second – only a second – he took his eyes from the fish.

And that's when it happened. The chinook made a lunge and just flipped that slippery, wooden-handled rod right out of his glove-covered grasp. Fish, rod and reel streaked for the bottom, and the angler was left counting the rings where he'd buried his tackle at sea.

It's not an unusual case. More than one fisherman has come home without his rod and reel because of a careless moment. But it doesn't have to happen to you.

Some fish are bigger than others, and stronger than others, and do what they do better than other fish do it. But they all do the same things. You have a better chance of avoiding trouble, putting more fish in the box — and returning to shore with more tackle — if you know what's likely to happen next.

A Deep Six and a plug-cut herring are what fooled this beautiful coho for John McCuistion.

There are several ways to catch salmon, and all of them have their adherents. One of the most popular and least expensive methods to gear up for is mooching. Why it's called that nobody knows, but it consists of simply dangling a bait, usually a herring or an anchovy, until a fish comes along and picks it up. Start with a good, medium-sized mooching rod of 8 to 9 feet, and a level-wind baitcasting reel of medium capacity. Neither has to be expensive. Daiwa, Eagle Claw and Lamiglas all make adequate mooching rods you can buy for about $50. Penn makes a very good mooching reel, the 109S, which sells for $30 to $40. It performs as well as many more expensive reels and, in fact, is favored by some anglers because when you crank the handle in free-spool it still retrieves line. That means you can flip the reel into free-spool and control a fish with pressure on the spool from your thumb, rather than setting the mechanical drag. Some anglers think that gives them a better feel for the fish. But catch a few the other way first, before you try this technique.

A little graphite in a rod's construction tends to make it more sensitive than plain fiberglass. As a rule of thumb, the more graphite, the greater the sensitivity. But be careful. A graphite rod doesn't have the resilience of glass for heavy work, and if you plan to use it for downrigger trolling, for example, you may be more likely to break it while trying to release your line from the downrigger.

Fill your reel with top-quality monofilament line of 12- to 15-pound test, and don't compromise on quality. Many anglers prefer brown or green line because it's least visible to the fish. Some tackle stores stock it in bulk, and you can take your reel in and have it filled for a fraction of what it would cost to buy the line on an individual spool.

Many beginners tend to buy gear that's too heavy. You want a rod of medium to medium-light action, with a sensitive tip, and a reel that doesn't look like it was made for billfish. The larger the reel, the more it comes between you and the fish when a fight is on. However, be sure that it has the capacity for a good 250 yards of whatever line you plan to put on it.

Beginners also tend to choose too heavy a line. Twelve- to 15-pound test is adequate in most circumstances. Remember, the heavier the test, the greater the diameter of the line, and the harder it will be to handle at greater depths and in stronger currents. You will need more weight to get it down, making your tackle less responsive.

With a lighter-weight line you may occasionally have to fire up the engine and chase a big chinook, but you're much more likely to have hooked him in the first place.

You'll need some crescent sinkers of 3 or 4 ounces, preferably the kind with a barrel swivel at one end and a chain swivel at the other. Some anglers use a crescent-shaped sinker with a small-diameter tube through it. You slide your line through the sinker and tie it off to a swivel on the far side. This allows the sinker to slide up and down your line.

That's all right for trolling, but it doesn't work well for mooching. Here's why. When you're mooching, a blackmouth often will pick up your bait as you let line out, and will swim toward the surface with it. If you're using a hollow sinker, the sinker will slide back along your line as the fish rises, keeping tension on the line and disguising the fact that a fish is bringing it toward you.

If you're using a sinker that's tied solidly to the end of your line, the premature slack when the fish picks it up will send you a signal. You'll reel as fast as you can, taking up slack, until you catch up with the surfacing fish. As soon as you feel his resistance, you'll sink the hooks home.

You'll need a 6-foot leader, tipped by a pair of hooks, one above the other about 2 1/2 inches apart. The upper hook often is one size larger than the trailing one.

Hooks of 2/0 and 3/0 are good for blackmouth most of the year, and for coho when they're running in from the ocean. For mature ocean chinook you might want to go to 4/0 and 5/0. Always, always sharpen your hooks before using them. A small, flat file works well.

Bait may be alive or dead, frozen or fresh. Usually it's dead, but live bait works wonderfully well. Even if you don't fish it alive, buy your bait fresh if you can. Frozen bait tends to be mushy, and doesn't stay on the hooks as well. Dip a bucket of water and put your bait in that, keeping it out of the sun if you can. The cold marine water will keep it in good condition all day, even though it may die in the bucket.

If you want, you can keep it alive in a minnow bucket, the kind that bass fishermen use. The bucket floats overboard, and you tie it off to a cleat. Many Northwest marinas carry these now. Use a plastic one for saltwater, of course, and don't forget to bring it into the boat before you run to a new fishing area.

Buy frozen herring only if you can't buy it or catch it fresh. On the fishing grounds, remove it from its package and put it in a bucket of seawater, just like fresh bait. The water will help thaw it, then will maintain it in as good a condition as possible. Don't let it sit in the sun in its plastic package, which will transfer heat to it. Salmon will not accept a tainted bait.

Meatline pole, center, is much heftier than mooching rods at left and right. Note the wheel on meat pole, which substitutes for guide. Reels on mooching rods are Daiwa Procaster, at left, and Penn 109S.

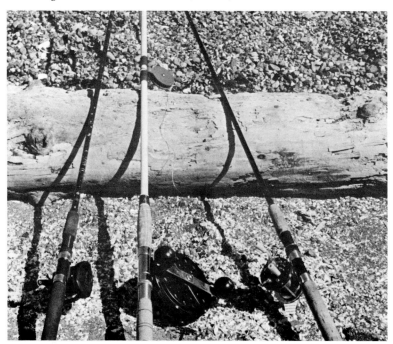

Place a whole or plug-cut herring on your hooks, and drop it over the side, holding your rod in one hand and stripping out line with the other. It's better to strip out line than it is to free-spool to the bottom, for a couple of reasons. For one, your gear will descend more slowly, and it's less likely your leader will wrap back around your main line.

For the other, you can count the pulls as you strip – something you always should do – and you'll know just where your bait is at all times. Figure a foot-and-a-half a pull. If your line should go slack short of the bottom, and you'll know how deep the bottom is by using your fish-finder, you'll know that something has taken the bait. Because you've counted the pulls, you'll also know at what depth the fish may be feeding, and you'll be able to return to that depth after the first fish is in the boat.

If you get all the way to the bottom without a hit, reel up quickly half a dozen turns, to keep from getting hung up. Let the current provide your bait with action. You can twitch it enticingly from time to time with the tip of the rod, but don't overdo it.

Coho often sock it and run with it right away. Chinook rarely do. A chinook, large or small, typically will tap it. You watch the tip of your rod, and when you see the tap, tap, tap evolve into a long, gentle pull, that's the time to sock it to him. And that's when he may explode.

If he's a fair-to-middlin'-sized fish, he's going to take some line on you, and you've got to be ready for it. Have your reel's drag pre-adjusted, so the fish can't put too much strain on your knots – the weakest links between you and him. You want him to be able to take line, but you want him to have to work for it.

If he's really a large one, he's going to take lots of line, and there's nothing to compare with the feeling that comes when you see that rotating spool getting smaller and smaller. If moderate pressure won't turn him, you're headed for trouble, because when he hits the end of that line it's going to pop like a thread.

All you can do is start up the engine and go after him. This is one time you'll be especially glad to have someone with you – your buddy, your wife, your brother-in-law, even – because it's tough to run a boat and play a big fish at the same time.

Have your companion take the tiller or the wheel and start out after the fish at about trolling speed. You'll see which way the line is pointed; there'll be no doubt about it. You play the fish just as you would if he didn't need chasing – holding your rod tip high and letting it absorb the shock, reeling when you can.

Eventually he'll stop or turn, and you stop your boat and fight him in the standard way. If you're fishing in Washington you'll be using barbless hooks, so never give him any slack. You don't have to be leaning back on the rod all the time, but you do have to maintain solid contact, enough to put a bow in your rod tip.

Let the fish fight the rod, not the line. Keep the tip up, so he has to bend it when he tugs. You pump the rod, bringing the fish gently closer on the upstroke, reeling to gain line on the downstroke. If your line goes slack you may have lost him. And you may not have. Start reeling as fast as you can, because he may be running toward the boat. It's not uncommon, and often you can catch up with him and re-establish contact. It's a risky period, though, during which he may throw the hook.

When you get the fish to the side of the boat, the fight is usually not over yet. Sight of the net seems to put new life in a tired fish, and he'll usually make at least one more line-stripping run. This is a critical time. Once they've gotten a fish to the boat, many beginners don't want it to run again. They clamp down on the spool, the panicked fish puts a strain on the knots, and it's goodbye salmon.

Fight the urge to do that. Your drag already is working all right or you wouldn't have gotten him this far. Let him run. Some will make two or three line-stripping runs from the side of the boat, each shorter than the last. Just keep the tension on, bring him back each time by pumping and reeling, and let him tell you when he's ready for the net.

When you can lead him with your rod, this way or that, slip your net into the water and lead him into it. Don't try to scoop him up, or you may lose him. And don't ever try to chase him with the net and catch him tail-first, or you'll surely lose him. Always net him head-first.

If he's a big one, and he tries to fight the net, lift him from the water with the net's handle straight up in the air. That closes off the mouth, and he can't escape.

When you bring the fish aboard, be very careful while he's thrashing around that you don't get a hook in your hand. If your hooks are as sharp as they should be they'll go right to the bone. Whack the fish sharply between the eyes with a hardwood club, and immediately cut a gill to bleed him and improve the quality of the meat. Of course, hold him over the side or over a bucket when you cut so you don't get blood all over the boat.

In many waters, size limits apply to various salmon, both minimum and maximum, depending on time and place and species. To be in compliance you need to be able to tell one kind from another, and to avoid the rough handling that can kill a fish it's helpful to be able to distinguish them while they're still in the water. If your fish is a sub-legal chinook, for example, carefully release it without netting it and without bringing it into the boat. That will increase its chances of survival significantly.

How do you tell them apart?

As you bring your salmon toward the net, estimate its size. If it looks as though it might be under the minimum size for chinook, look at its sides. If you see a purple iridescence, it is a chinook. As the fish comes closer alongside, you can glance inside its mouth. If it's a chinook, it will be black where the teeth protrude from the gums. If it's a coho, the entire inside of the mouth will be gray. Look at the tip of its lower jaw. A chinook's will be pointed. A coho's will be round.

You also can look at the tail. A chinook will have spots on both the upper and lower lobes. A coho will have spots just on the upper lobe.

* * *

Chapter Four

Trolling

———————————————————————

I WAS PEERING OVER THE BOW OF MY 15-FOOTER, steering on a distant landmark, when I heard a soft "Thwunk" from the stern.

Looking over my shoulder toward the downrigger, I could see my fiberglass fishing rod standing nearly straight in its holder on the gunwale, only its supple tip curving rearward. The monofilament line stretched far behind the boat, entering the water at an acute angle. Fish on!

I jumped from my seat and reached the rod in one step, slipping it from its holder and taking a couple of turns on the reel to make sure the line was tight. Then I set the hook — hard — and now the fish was really on!

It happened in Puget Sound off Point Defiance, not far from Tacoma, and a few minutes later a chunky, 12-pound blackmouth was flopping in the bottom of the boat. It might not have been, had I not been paying attention to what my ears had told me. It's not unusual to hear evidence of a fish before you see it when you're trolling for Pacific salmon.

There are four ways you can troll for these fish. All are effective, but some more so than others, and some more so under certain circumstances.

Some popular salmon-trolling plugs. Clockwise, from top right, they are a Tomic 109, Tomic 128, six-inch Silver Horde No. 1, and 5½-inch Silver Horde Ace Hi No. 19.

Mooching Gear

The first is with mooching gear. This is particularly effective for young resident coho in the late spring. For this you simply troll a whole or plug-cut herring 50 or 60 feet behind the boat on regular mooching hooks tied below a crescent sinker of 1 to 5 ounces. The size of the weight and the speed of the boat determine the depth at which the herring is fished, and young coho often will come right to the top to grab it. So will small blackmouth.

You may troll with the rod in your hand, or in a holder at the rail, and you strike as soon as you see or feel a hit. Generally, a striking fish will hook itself, and your job is simply to give it no slack as you slide the rod from its holder. Some anglers prefer lures over bait for this type of fishing, eliminating the crescent sinker and pulling the lure behind a small barrel sinker of the type used in freshwater fishing – or, in some cases, behind a couple of split shot. The No. 50 Hot Shot is very effective, especially in green.

Don't let out too much line with this method, particularly in crowded waters, because the more you put out the greater its resistance against the water, and the higher your bait or lure tends to ride. And few things are as annoying as a guy with a couple of hundred feet of monofilament trailing behind his boat in a large sportfishing fleet.

The major problem with mooching gear is that it is nearly impossible to get a trolled bait or lure down to where larger fish wait to take it. You can solve this problem with a planer.

Planers

A planer is a triangular or round piece of plastic with a device for changing its center of balance so that when it's being trolled, it is lowering its nose into the current and diving, like a deep-running lure. When a fish hits, the center of balance changes, and the planer provides little resistance to the angler as he fights the fish.

Used with whole or plug-cut herring, planers are particularly effective on mature silver salmon, and have helped put many a lunker in the boat up and down the Pacific coast.

My own preference is for the Les Davis Deep Six, and I always use size No. 2. I prefer it to its major competitor, the Pink Lady, because the Deep Six release mechanism is adjustable.

A planer growing in popularity is the Dipsy Diver. It has a means of changing its center of balance not only front to back, in order to dive, but also side to side in order to take a lure out to the left or the right of the boat.

Planers and flashers are popular for West Coast salmon fishing. On log at top is a Deep Six planer, which will take trolled lines down for anglers without downriggers. Below log, top center, is a Dipsy Diver. It does the same as a Deep Six, but also has a weight which can be set to take it to port or to starboard. This allows anglers to run more lines off a stern by separating them in the water. On left and right at bottom are Hot Spot flashers, very popular in the Northwest in all sorts of trolling situations, and which rotate ahead of the bait or lure. At bottom center is a dodger, which spins instead of rotates. It often is used with fresh bait.

By shifting a weight on the bottom of the Dipsy Diver, an angler can run some lines far to each side of the boat while others are trolled directly astern. That permits the trolling of more lines than otherwise would be possible.

Always attach about a foot of heavy monofilament to the barrel swivel at the rear of your planer, and finish off with a top-quality ball-bearing swivel at the end of that. When you fish, attach your baited mooching hooks to the ball-bearing swivel. If you tied a plug-cut herring directly to the barrel swivel that comes with the planer, your leader would twist and break.

As with any other kind of trolling, planer trolling is a matter of time, place, speed and depth. With your boat at trolling speed, strip out enough line to get your bait to the depth at which you think the fish are feeding. This may be anywhere from 15 to 45 pulls, and often is far closer to 15 than to 45. Silvers usually feed in the top 20 or 30 feet of water, and you generally don't have to go deep to find them.

Place your rod in a holder, and keep one eye on it. When a silver hits, there'll be no mistaking it.

Downriggers

Downriggers are for going deeper yet, and for fishing heavier terminal tackle — the kind whose own weight would keep tripping a planer's release mechanism if you tried to use it with a Deep Six.

A downrigger is simple in principle. It consists of a wire line, usually braided, on a reel with a crank handle. The reel has a counter for keeping track of the amount of line that is out. At the end of the wire is a weight, usually 10 pounds or more. You attach your monofilament fishing line to the wire line, by means of a quick-release mechanism, then lower both over the side of the boat. The heavy weight on the wire line takes it down to the depth you desire. When a fish hits, your monofilament is released from the wire, and you play the fish on it alone, with no weight between you.

Downriggers are mounted on a boat's gunwale, sometimes on the transom. Obviously, you need a long enough shaft between the reel and the pulley at the end of the shaft to clear any obstructions the boat provides. But don't think that a long shaft is necessarily better than a short one. Remember, the longer the shaft, the greater the strain it transmits to the gunwale, particularly if you happen to get hung up.

Here's how you rig for fishing. With your boat moving at trolling speed, toss your bait or lure over the stern and let out about 30 feet of monofilament. Then, with your downrigger line over the side and the weight just reaching the water, attach your monofilament to the downrigger line. With your rod in one hand, loosen the downrigger brake with the other and lower the weight in a controlled manner, letting out monofilament as the downrigger line submerges.

When you have reached the depth at which you want to fish, tighten the brake, then reel up half a dozen turns on the monofilament to put a good bend in the rod, and slip the rod into a holder. The bend in the rod should prevent the fish from getting too much slack when he pops the monofilament from its release mechanism.

When the line pops loose you sometimes will hear it, as I did that day off Point Defiance. But you can't count on it, so glance at it frequently. When your gear is attached to the wire line, your rod will be sharply arched, its tip pointed down, and your monofilament will enter the water next to the boat. When the line has popped loose the rod will be straighter, and the line will enter the water far behind the boat.

When a fish has hit, get the rod from its holder as quickly as possible and sink the hook home. And don't stop the boat until then. After the fish is solidly hooked, you can throw the motor into neutral. If you're fishing with a friend, he should pop his gear loose from the downrigger and reel it in, then should retrieve the downrigger line, if possible, before helping you net the fish. If you're fishing alone, this is when it's nice to have an electric downrigger. Turn the switch to retrieve, and get your wire line out of the water before your fish comes close enough to wrap the monofilament around it. If the lines become tangled, a good-sized fish almost always will break off.

Anglers troll a variety of gear from a downrigger – bait, spoons, flies and lures. One of the most effective combinations is the flasher and hoochie. A hoochie is a plastic squid, a few inches long, and a flasher is an oblong piece of metal or plastic with a reflective surface. The flasher rotates in front of the hoochie, and attracts a fish's attention to it. When a hoochie is attached properly, its leader about 2 1/2 times the length of the flasher's blade, the flasher's rotation gives it a stop-and-go action, causing its skirts to swirl enticingly.

Hoochies come in a variety of colors, and in finishes from plain to spangled to luminescent. Color can be critical. One day the fish may prefer blue, another day green, the day after that white. You should carry a variety. They're least expensive if you buy them without hooks and add your own snelled mooching hooks. Metallic skirts, made of aluminum foil tied to a plastic head, can be inserted when you install the hooks, to make the hoochie more appealing.

Abe & Al produces a popular metal flasher. Gold Star makes another, which is stronger and less prone to stretching out of shape when a big fish socks your lure. One of the most popular among commercial fishermen in the Northwest is the Canadian-made Hot Spot, a colored, plastic flasher with a metal reflector strip on each side. I use Hot Spots almost exclusively, and find that red is most effective.

A coho fly can be used behind a flasher in the same way as a hoochie. Again, color can be important.

Bait can be fished alone off a downrigger or behind a dodger. A dodger is an oblong metal reflector, usually smaller than a flasher and with fewer bends. Rather than rotating, as a flasher does, a dodger spins. It doesn't impart any action to the bait, but attracts attention.

Every good tackle store sells a variety of downrigger releases. They're all designed to attach securely to the downrigger and to hold the angler's monofilament line just tightly enough to keep it at the depth where the angler wants it. Each is adjustable, so an angler can make it just tight enough to keep it from releasing prematurely. A solid strike should be enough to pop it loose.

Some mechanisms attach to the downrigger weight itself. But I prefer the kind that attach to the wire above the weight. That way, I can "stack" lines, running two or more lures off one downrigger, depending upon how many anglers I have in the boat.

When you stack lines, attach one about 20 feet higher than the other, and run the lures or bait out varying distances behind the boat. When stacking, attach the bottom line first. Loosen the downrigger brake and lower the downrigger weight 20 feet, then attach the next line, and so forth.

Commonly used metal jigs, all effective on salmon, are, from left, Point Wilson Dart in herring style, Point Wilson Dart in candlefish style, Dungeness Stinger and Buzz Bomb.

If your partner is running the boat and you are handling both rods, you can keep one in your hand while lowering the gear. Put the reel on free-spool and keep your thumb on the spool as the line plays out, to keep from getting a crow's nest. Place the other rod in its holder, the gears of the reel engaged and its drag set very lightly.

The resistance offered by the drag will prevent the line from tangling as it plays out. As soon as the gear has reached the proper depth, retighten the drag.

How deep should you fish a downrigger? That depends. You want your bait or lure to be where the fish are feeding, but first you have to find them. For some reason, 90 and 120 feet are magic numbers for chinook salmon. Many anglers will start at 90 and, if they don't find fish in a few minutes, will drop to 120.

Big chinook often feed near the bottom, and a good method is to lower the downrigger to the bottom, then crank up a few turns to clear any obstructions. You have to keep a close eye on your depthfinder when fishing this way, to avoid hanging up. And you have to pay particular attention to which way you're drifting when you're fighting a fish if you haven't had time to retrieve the downrigger line. Those weights are expensive.

Keep varying the depth until you find where the fish are working. Even then, you should not troll for more than about twenty minutes without cranking in your gear to check it. Often you may be pulling an undersized fish without realizing it, one too small to pop your line loose. Or, you may be pulling some kelp, in which case you're wasting your time.

To pop loose your gear from a downrigger, remove your rod from its holder, point the rod tip at the spot where your line enters the water, and reel until the line is as tight as you can get it. Then pull straight back, your rod making a straight line with the monofilament. Don't whip the rod, as though striking a fish, because you may break it.

Whenever you fish with a downrigger, it's best to use a glass rod. A rod with lots of graphite may be too brittle.

Meatlines

Meatlining is a method of trolling with a short, stout fiberglass rod built with pulleys rather than guides, with a heavy weight, usually 8 to 10 pounds, and with a large, direct-drive reel. The reel is filled with wire line, usually braided, but sometimes solid. Some anglers say they prefer the solid line because it doesn't fray. But if it kinks it will break. Braided line will not.

The difference between meatlining and downrigging is that with meatlining you attach your lure permanently to the wire. When a fish strikes, both it and you must fight the weight as well as each other. Why is it called meatlining? Because it's efficient. It puts a lot of meat on the table.

Meatline fishermen generally pull a plug or a flasher and hoochie. You rig by running your wire line to a heavy-duty, three-way swivel. To the bottom of the swivel you attach three or four feet of heavy Dacron line, and to the far end of that you attach your weight.

To the middle part of the three-way swivel you attach a heavy- duty rubber snubber – everything's heavy-duty in meatlining – and to the far end of the snubber you tie your flasher or lure by means of about 30 feet of large-test monofilament. When a big fish hits, the snubber absorbs the shock.

You fish a meatline the same as a downrigger, except you have no counter on your reel, so you have to estimate how much line is out. Many anglers like to fish it right on the bottom, literally bumping it along. You have to pay attention to the bottom configuration, though, or you're going to lose some weights.

It's surprising how well a stubby little meat pole will telegraph a hit. A fair-sized fish will have it bouncing in its holder – which must be as heavy-duty as everything else in meatlining. Many anglers use holders of brass or steel, because the popular plastic ones won't stand the strain.

A lot of anglers also attach a bell to the tip of the pole. That way they can pay more attention to running their boat and still know immediately when a fish hits.

Fighting a fish on a meatline is not a pretty thing to watch. It's just a matter of horsing it in. But it gets a little tricky when that three-way swivel reaches the rod tip. You still have 30 feet of monofilament between you and the fish, which you have to bring in hand-over-hand. A last-minute run can be a problem now, and if you're going to lose the fish, this probably is when it will happen.

* * *

Chapter Five

Neah Bay

—————————————

PEEL AWAY ALL OF THE MYSTERY THAT envelops salmon fishing, and you're left with one basic principle. To catch fish, you have to be where fish are.

It couldn't have been impressed upon me any more clearly that late-summer day at the Strait of Juan de Fuca's western entrance, where the Pacific Ocean stretches an arm inland between Washington state and Canada's Vancouver Island.

We were fishing out of Neah Bay on the Makah Indian Reservation, the last town on the strait before you reach Cape Flattery on Washington's northwest tip. It's a good place to intercept ocean fish that funnel through the strait toward their natal rivers farther east. But it had been frustrating. We'd been dragging cut-plug herring through the rips for hours, and hadn't been able to find a fish.

It was late August — coho time — but those big, hooknose silvers were nowhere to be found. We'd worked our way as far west as the Whistler Buoy, about a mile and a quarter northwest of Tatoosh Island and just outside the mouth of the strait. The Whistler is usually a sure thing this time of year, giving up limit after easy limit, but we couldn't raise so much as a tap. We were fishing with planers, and we knew we were doing it right. It was only a matter of finding a school.

Just then Al Seda, one of my companions, looked out over the rolling swells to the west and saw what we'd been searching for — gulls, hundreds of them, circling and swooping, three or four miles away. Seda, operator of the Big Salmon Resort at Neah Bay, knew what that meant. The birds had found bait, and where there was bait there was bound to be salmon.

We ran to the spot, tossed a couple of planers over the stern, and nearly instantly had two hookups. From that moment on, silvers hammered our bait as fast as we could get it into the water, sometimes grabbing it right next to the boat and snapping our leaders in two. Sometimes they leaped and contorted as only coho can, throwing our barbless hooks before we could bring them to the net. We re-rigged, re-baited and fought coho for about 15 wonderful minutes, and then our limits were in the box. We'd been fishing all morning without result. Then, once the action had started, it was over in a quarter-hour.

That's the way it can be with silvers, and the Neah Bay area is one of the prime places on the Pacific coast to go after them.

The western end of the strait has been kind of a no-man's land when it comes to fishery-management practices, with the Washington Department of Fisheries seemingly unable to decide whether it's part of the ocean, where allocations of fish are tightly apportioned, or part of the inland waters, where rules are more liberal. That has led to some volatile management practices and to a lot of uncertainty over opening and closing dates, bag limits and other regulations in the waters from Tatoosh Island east to the Sekiu River.

The town of Neah Bay itself provides the best access to this area, and launching and moorage are available, for a fee, at several of the resorts there. The bay is protected from ocean swells by a rock jetty that extends most of the way across its entrance.

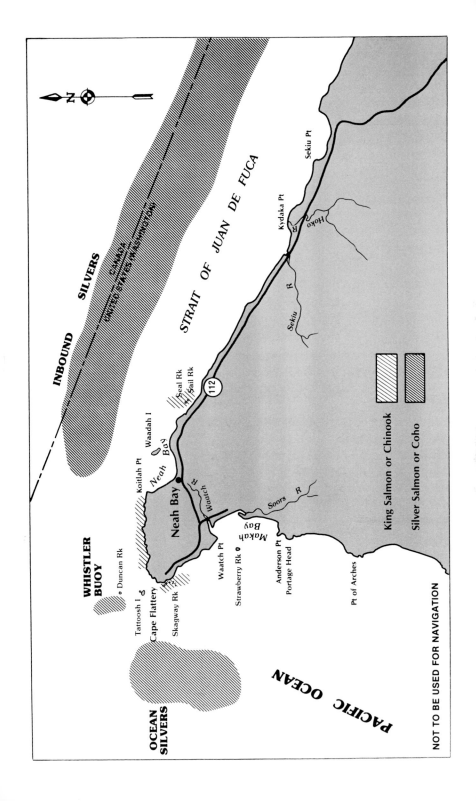

Whether sitting on the tramsom or standing farther forward in the boat, Ed Mares finds an extension handle makes handling easier.

If the area opens early enough, it can be excellent in March and April for feeder chinook which are working their way toward the ocean. These are typically 8 to 12 pounds, with some into the middle and high teens. They tend to be scattered, so it's mainly a downrigger fishery, because you've got to troll to find them. Use a flasher and hoochie, and fish just off the bottom in about 180 feet of water. These are outbound salmon, so fish the ebb tide – the stronger the better. One that starts about daylight is ideal.

Start at Waadah Island at the entrance to Neah Bay, and motor northward until you hit a depth of 30 or 40 fathoms. Then turn east and troll along that contour line to Seal Rock or to Sail Rock, a distance of a couple of miles. You'll stay about one mile off the beach. Then you can turn and troll back with the current.

About this time, Puget Sound coho are passing through the area in huge numbers on their way to the ocean, where they will spend the summer feeding and growing just west of the mouth of the strait. These coho average only 16 to 22 inches now, and if you want to avoid them you have to fish deep.

Weather can be a problem this time of year. The wind

can whip the water for days, keeping boats on the beach, and sometimes a trip can be spent just waiting in vain for a chance to fish.

By the middle of May the outbound chinook are gone, and the coho are, too.

When the first inbound chinook reach Washington's northern ocean beaches, they rarely come right inside the strait. So fishing generally remains poor until the ocean season opens. About the last week of June or the first week of July, the first runs of fall chinook will be gathering off Skagway Rocks and Makah Bay, just south of Tatoosh on the ocean side of the cape.

A lot of anglers mooch for them with 3 or 4 ounces of lead. Others troll with flasher and hoochie, or flasher and bait. The fish will be 3 or 4 pounds short of their spawning weight, and will be feeding voraciously, so just about anything works. They'll continue to congregate here into August.

At Skagway, about a mile south of Tatoosh, rocks stick out about half a mile from the beach. Behind them is a sort of bay, and a popular gathering place for candlefish. The bottom comes up from 30 or 35 fathoms to about 10 fathoms in the bay, and big kings move right into those shallows after the bait. Anglers anchor there to mooch for the kings. Skagway tends to be best on a tide change, and generally on low slack. But it can vary.

As soon as that first group of fall chinook arrives, a few of the fish begin moving into the strait. From then into August, more and more chinook will be coming inside. Many anglers like to fish for them there, where they don't have to contend with the ocean's heavy swells. Fish the tide changes in the strait, and stay close to the beach. High slack can be especially productive.

Meanwhile, silvers are available in the ocean all summer long. These are the fish that moved out through the strait in April and May. As a rule, you motor 3 to 4 miles off the coast, and you're into them. These fish, 16 to 22 inches long when they came through the strait, have been stuffing themselves with krill in the ocean, and they're gaining a pound every couple of weeks.

About the middle of July, you can begin taking them on coho flies, trolled on the surface with no weight. Blue is a productive color here. Locate a school, strip out 20 or 30 feet of line, and troll fast – so that the fly skips on top of the water. Then stand back. The fish will boil up and slam it right in the boat's wake.

About the middle of August, the silvers that have been putting on pounds in the ocean start moving into the strait, and you can go out in the rips beyond Waadah Island and catch them with flies, with cut-plug herring behind planers, or with cut-plugs and 3 or 4 ounces of lead. This action continues until about the middle of September, providing a month of often incredible fishing.

A lot of these silvers run 10 to 12 pounds, some as large as 20, and the action can be so good that anglers sort for larger fish, releasing any under the 10-pound mark. These silvers are hungry, and nearly anyone can catch them. Some anglers who can't catch chinook, in fact, go after the coho and make it look easy.

One other thing is happening at this time. Most migrating fall chinook will have moved on by the first or second week of August. But some of Washington's finest big-fish angling occurs in this part of the strait in September.

From Neah Bay all the way to Sekiu, anglers will be boating fish in the 40s, the 50s and even the 60s. It's just a trickle of fish, but their size makes the effort worthwhile.

Most of them probably will be caught on a flasher and hoochie or flasher and bait, not far from the beach. A trolled plug can be effective, provided you use a large one and troll it deep and slow. Some anglers use spinner baits cut from the sides of large herring and fished behind 2 or 3 ounces of lead.

If you're fishing herring, keep in mind that these big fish are not hard strikers. The pick-up may be subtle. When you think you feel it you should strip off a pull or two of line. Give the fish a chance to gum the bait a little before you set the hook.

Then look out!

* * *

Chapter Six

Sekiu to Pillar Point

———————————————

YOU ROLL OUT OF YOUR SLEEPING BAG EARLY at Sekiu, when the summer sky is still black. By 4 in the morning the whole town is stirring, like an anthill that's been kicked by some giant boot. Already you can see the running lights of small boats moving slowly out of Clallam Bay, feeling their way in the dark into the Strait of Juan de Fuca, where they'll set up drifts to intercept big king salmon at first light.

If you're camping, you walk to the washroom, and find a line stretching out of the building and around the corner. Doors bang, people curse and laugh, and another day is under way. The bait shops are open, spilling light from their windows, and people head for their brightness like moths. Fresh herring is what they're after, and a brisk trade is going on in little plastic bagsful of them.

There's a special feeling here, a special excitement. Your senses are super-sharp, despite the early hour, and you know that there's potential for great things — for the kind of day, perhaps, on which fish stories come true.

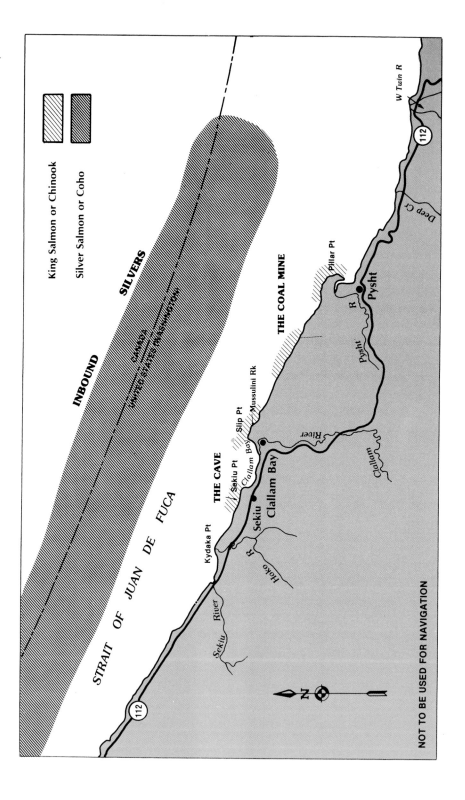

King Salmon or Chinook

Silver Salmon or Coho

INBOUND

SILVERS

CANADA
UNITED STATES (WASHINGTON)

STRAIT OF JUAN DE FUCA

THE CAVE

THE COAL MINE

Kydaka Pt

Sekiu Pt

Slip Pt

Mussulini Rk

Pillar Pt

Pysht

W Twin R

112

Deep Cr

Sekiu River

Hoko R

Sekiu

Clallam Bay

Clallam Bay

Clallam River

Pysht R

Pysht River

N

112

NOT TO BE USED FOR NAVIGATION

Darkness still hangs heavily when you reach the float where you've moored your boat. You give your engine a couple of minutes' warm-up, then cast off and move slowly out of the basin and toward the strait, straining your eyes for deadheads in the water. At the end of the bay is Sekiu Point, and as you turn the corner into the strait you can't believe your eyes.

To the west as far as you can see, it seems, are running lights – hundreds of them – bobbing quietly in the dark. The boats are gathered off the caves, a popular mooching spot, where anglers will try their early morning luck. If the first half hour of daylight doesn't produce a big king, many will move on, into the rips, in search of silvers.

Summer isn't the only time the fishing's good at Sekiu, however. In January, Indian commercial troll fishermen take some nice blackmouth here. Occasionally a sport fisherman shows up to participate, but it's usually not until February that anglers really begin to trickle in. And then it's only a relative handful.

On through March, local waters continue to produce blackmouth, mostly 5 to 7 pounds, fish which usually take a bait or a lure readily when weather permits boats to venture out.

At this time of year, too, good fishing can be found off the caves, and from there to Eagle Bay, about 3 miles to the west. It also can be good off Slip Point, at the eastern entrance to Clallam Bay, and from there to Mussolini Rock, an outcropping just east of Slip. A lot of anglers like heavy gear at this season. Meatlines are popular for pulling a flasher and a coho fly, and usually are fished deep.

If you are driving very far to get here, you want to allow several days at Sekiu if you can, however, because of Washington's unstable winter weather. In a typical week you might get four days of fishing, and the rest of the time storms might keep you on the beach.

By April, the blackmouth have grown much larger. Fishing is productive now all the way from Eagle Bay to the coal mine, about 6 miles east of Sekiu. By mid-April, and on through May, you will see more and more chinook in the

12-to 18-pound range. Many anglers use downriggers, pulling flashers and flies. By June, many switch to hoochies.

The fish are close to the rocks now, in 40 or 50 feet of water, and fishing is good around the caves, at Sekiu Point and at Slip Point. The coal mine can be excellent, too, especially in the evenings through June and July.

From late June into August, kings from 30 to 50 pounds are arriving from the ocean, and are not uncommon. They're still tight along the beach, and you'll find them in the same places you were taking smaller fish in May.

But nothing lasts forever. By the middle of August, kings are becoming scarce around Sekiu, and ocean silvers are starting to show. You've got to go offshore to find the silvers, into the shipping lanes 4 to 6 miles from the beach. From the middle of August to early September, silvers run mostly 4 to 8 pounds, but by mid-September they've undergone a change. Now they're typically 10 to 14 pounds, with a few into the 20s. And in a good year they'll continue passing this area as late as October.

Many anglers from Washington's metropolitan areas never drive as far as Sekiu, however. They headquarter near Pillar Point, 10 miles to the east, and fish east and west of there for both coho and chinook. Like Sekiu, Pillar Point is a blackmouth show from late November until late March or early April, with fish running mostly 6 to 8 pounds, and occasionally into the teens.

In April, the first spring fish arrive. You can get them two ways. You can troll a herring, a hoochie or a spoon − slow and deep − or you can mooch the holes around the point. Pillar is mainly a mooching area by tradition, and a place where you don't have to go very deep. Water 30 to 50 feet deep often holds very nice fish.

One productive hole is located on the eastern side of Pillar, where the Pysht River empties into the strait. Another lies just to the west of the point, where a little reef comes out. Go around the reef, east to west, then back along its far side, and there's a hole on the western edge. Another hole lies farther west, between Pillar Point and Codfish Bay, and another lies in your path as you enter the bay. All are places where fish gather.

As you come out of Codfish Bay going west, the water drops off deeply. It's an excellent spot for chinook, right in close — no more than 100 yards from the beach. About 4 miles west of Pillar, halfway between it and Clallam Bay, is the coal mine, where boats from Pillar and Sekiu often meet.

Anglers take a lot of chinook to the east of Pillar, as well, off the mouth of the West Twin River, about 6 1/2 miles up the strait.

By late May or early June, the Elwha River run of kings has arrived. This is a unique genetic strain that shares a tendency to grow. And to grow. Each year, this run provides fish into the 50s, sometimes larger. Mooching is most effective for these, especially along the edges of the kelp, in water to about 60 feet deep.

Action sometimes undergoes a brief lull near Pillar in June, then in the latter part of the month a fresh run arrives. Kings continue to come through in waves in July and August.

Sometime in August, the first ocean silvers reach the point. Their runs usually continue through September and into October. By late September these are big fish, often running into the middle and high teens.

A final run of kings — white-meated fish — shows up at Pillar around the end of September, after many anglers have gone home. Some of these weigh well into the 40s. You can get them by mooching the standard spots. Anglers fishing the Sekiu area may launch and moor, for a fee, at any of several resorts in the town of Sekiu. Keep in mind, however, that the facilities sometimes are jammed, particularly on holiday weekends.

Those who prefer to headquarter near Pillar can launch and moor at the Silver King Resort there, in a tiny boat basin protected by a breakwater. Sometimes moorage fills up quickly at Silver King, however, at the height of the season.

* * *

Chapter Seven

Port Angeles to Port Townsend

NOTHING ABOUT THE STRIKE INDICATED IT was anything out of the ordinary. It was mushy, uncertain, a tentative tap on the way down by what might have been an undersize blackmouth.

I'd been stripping line out when it happened, trying to get a plug-cut herring to the bottom on the 20-fathom line just outside Ediz Hook at Port Angeles.

The pick-up had been so subtle I'd almost missed it. I started reeling as fast as possible, and when I finally made contact with the fish, I leaned back and gave the rod a hard pull. That's when the salmon took off.

My rod doubled over, and my reel started humming in a way that's music to an angler's ears.

The fish, stung by the barbless hook, headed west along the beach, in the general direction of Sekiu and the Pacific Ocean, peeling off line and taking it smack through the middle of what looked like the largest armada assembled since the Normandy invasion. The only thing to do was keep the pressure on and wait for him to turn. But this guy didn't.

I watched in dismay as the line melted from my reel, getting closer to the bare metal, the fish on the other end of it getting farther and farther into the fleet.

My companion started our engine, and kicked it gently into gear. We followed the salmon into the crowd, my partner steering a course among the other craft, and me standing in the stern trying to gain line. From time to time I took my hand from the reel to wave off boats that were about to cross my line. Most of them paid heed. Some of them didn't, and my language would have raised blisters on a horsehide glove.

As luck would have it, though, the fish was deep enough that the outboard props whirring back and forth across the line failed to reach it. And about when I began to think the contest would go on forever, the fish finally ran out of steam and came to the side of the boat. My partner slipped the net around him and we hauled him aboard − 24 1/2 pounds of nickel-bright chinook salmon.

We were delighted, but not surprised. It was July, and the waters off Port Angeles often are alive with big chinook at that time of year. The size of the fleet was testimony to the fact that this was no secret.

Fishing can be good around Port Angeles at any time. In winter it's blackmouth that bring the locals out. They find them in the Winter Hole, about a mile off the Crown Zellerbach mill; and on the humps beyond the hole. Sometimes the waters off Freshwater Bay will give up blackmouth, and at times they'll follow the baitfish right into Port Angeles Harbor, where anglers jig for them beneath the log booms.

July and August mean runs of mature ocean chinook, and the fishing then can be superb. Like migrating chinook everywhere, these tend to follow the beach, and the best place to find them is right outside the hook.

You can launch at the ramp on the tip of the hook near the Thunderbird Boat House, or at the West Boat Haven ramp near downtown. Both launching and parking are free, and parking is more than ample, particularly on the hook. Bait is available both places.

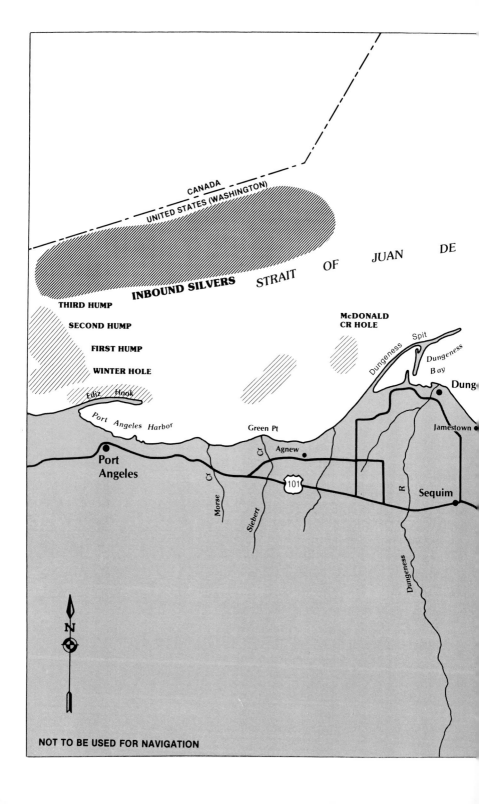

CANADA
UNITED STATES (WASHINGTON)

STRAIT OF JUAN DE

INBOUND SILVERS

THIRD HUMP

SECOND HUMP

FIRST HUMP

WINTER HOLE

McDONALD
CR HOLE

Dungeness Spit

Dungeness Bay

Dung

Ediz Hook

Port Angeles Harbor

Green Pt

Agnew

Jamestown

Port
Angeles

Cr

101

R

Sequim

Morse

Siebert

Cr

Dungeness

N

NOT TO BE USED FOR NAVIGATION

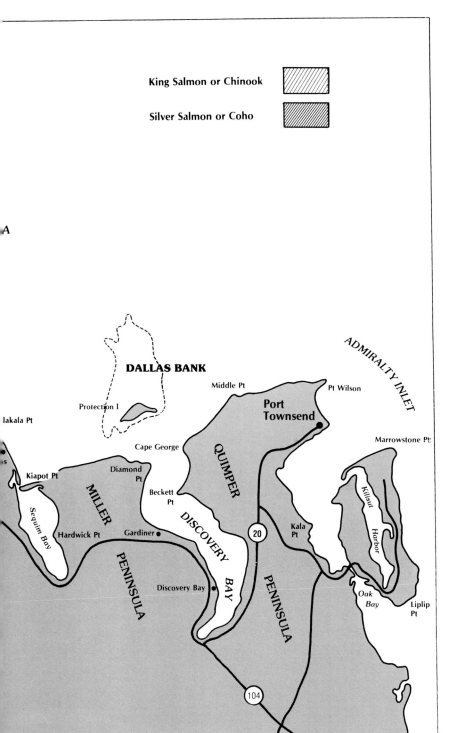

King Salmon or Chinook

Silver Salmon or Coho

A

DALLAS BANK

ADMIRALTY INLET

Middle Pt
Pt Wilson

Port
Townsend

Protection I

lakala Pt

Marrowstone Pt

Cape George

QUIMPER

Kiapot Pt

Diamond
Pt

Beckett
Pt

Kilisut
Harbor

MILLER

Sequim Bay

DISCOVERY BAY

Hardwick Pt

Gardiner

20

Kala
Pt

PENINSULA

Discovery Bay

PENINSULA

Oak
Bay

Liplip
Pt

104

As always, it's best if you can pick a day when the tidal exchange is moderate. You need to fish when the fish are running, however, and if that happens to be a day with strong tides you'll need to fish around the high and low slacks.

The key to ocean-run chinook at Port Angeles in July and August is that 20-fathom line. Find it, drop your herring to the bottom, then reel up a couple of turns and drift the line either east or west along the hook, depending on which way the tide is running. If it's very early morning, still dark on the water, start at 12 to 15 fathoms, and go deeper as the sun gains strength. If the 20-fathom line is not productive, work all the way to 40, keeping your herring always just off the bottom.

At different times the fish will concentrate at different places along the hook – near the Coast Guard station, the pilot house or other landmarks. Channel 21 is the local CB station, and often it will tell you where and when the bite is on.

If the water is crowded off the hook, don't neglect the Winter Hole, even in July or August. Especially in July or August. Migratory chinook often rest there. It's worth a try at any time, especially on an ebb tide, if you can bring yourself to run past the big fish you suspect must be holding off the hook.

To find it, set a course between 250 and 260 degrees, magnetic, from the end of the hook, and run until you pass the Crown Zellerbach plant. About half a mile beyond the mill the bottom will pop up from 35 or 40 fathoms to about 10. Turn back to the drop-off, and you're over the hole.

The area known as the First Hump forms the seaward side of the Winter Hole. To find it, go northeast out of the hole until the bottom comes up. Then bear north until you drop over the far edge. The first gully west of the Crown Zellerbach plant is on a line with the northeast corner of the First Hump.

To find the Second Hump, go northwest from the First Hump until the red-and-white telephone tower on Angeles Point lines up with a hayfield in Eden Valley, behind it. Keeping the two in line, proceed toward the tower until the bottom comes up to about 10 fathoms from 35. Turn back to the dropoff, and you're at the edge of the Hump.

The Third Hump is still farther northwest. Go until you're due north of the Port Angeles landfill, then turn and approach it until the tallest stack at the Crown Zellerbach mill, to your southeast, lines up with Mount Pleasant, the highest hill in the Olympic Range just east of Port Angeles. Right about there the bottom pops up to 30 fathoms from about 75, and you're over the spot.

You should be at the Winter Hole about an hour before high slack, and fish through the change. When the bite ceases there, run for the Second Hump. When the bite stops again, run for the Third. As low slack approaches, reverse the procedure. Be back at the Winter Hole by low slack.

Experienced Port Angeles anglers try to be in position at tide changes. As the change approaches, remember: If the fish aren't feeding yet, they are going to be. So be on the Humps and be patient. Don't be caught screaming around on the change, and miss the bite entirely.

If the Hook and the Hole and the Hump aren't producing, you can run in the other direction to Green Point and beyond. Sometimes Green Point is excellent in the summer, and sometimes nothing is happening there at all. It's seldom a compromise. A wide, shallow shelf extends seaward from the point, as it does all along this part of the Strait, and you have to move out far enough to find the drop-off, about 3 1/4 miles off the beach. Salmon, halibut and lingcod offer a mixed bag for anglers here. On an ebb tide, start your drift at about 30 fathoms, and let the current carry you southwest to about 22 fathoms. Take long drifts until you locate the fish, then concentrate on the area where they're feeding. On a flood tide, start at about 24 fathoms, and drift northeast to the 32 fathom mark.

A few words of caution: Sea-going freighters steam right through this area to and from the pilot station at Port Angeles, and you have to watch out for them all the time. And, when the wind rises, waves can stack up on the shelf off the point, making it dangerous for small craft.

Beyond the point, eastward up the Strait a few miles, is Dungeness Spit. Out from the base of the spit is the McDonald Creek Hole, a deep-water area that pops up onto a flat like the Winter Hole. You fish it the same as the Winter Hole, dropping your bait down along the ledge. Like the Winter Hole, McDonald Creek is best on the ebb.

Port Angeles is a place where many local anglers would rather jig than mooch, because dogfish can be such a problem, and they take a lot of big salmon that way. Mooch-A-Jigs are popular, and so are Point Wilson Darts. Sometimes it's the herring-style darts that are hot, sometimes the candlefish. Check the style and the color that are working when you're there.

If you're jigging, drop the lure to the bottom, reel up a few turns, and work the rod tip gently up and down two or three feet at a time. Don't lift the tip too high, because when you get a hit you need room to strike. The fish will nearly always take it on the downward flutter, by the way, not on the upward stroke.

August is when migratory coho start to show in strength, and you'll find them out in the rips. Plan on running as many as 5 or 6 miles offshore, and expect to do some prospecting before you zero in on them.

Look for birds and monitor your CB to find out where the schools may be.

Coho fishing here means trolling. Downriggers work well with flasher and fly, and if the fish are feeding near the surface you can take them on a plug-cut herring behind 3 or 4 ounces of lead. Don't overlook planers like the Deep Six, the Pink Lady or the Dipsy Diver. They work extremely well.

Up the Strait beyond Dungeness Spit is Port Townsend, and its famous Midchannel Bank. The bank is a lot closer to the Puget Sound metropolitan area than are Port Angeles and the places beyond, and is a wonderful place to fish for winter blackmouth. Summertime angling is even better than what's available in winter, however, because in the summer migrating fish stop to feed here.

To find the bank, follow a compass heading of 60 degrees

from the downtown Port Townsend area until, off the northern end of Marrowstone Island, the bottom comes up to 8 or 10 fathoms. Bear north until the bottom drops off, and fish along the eastern edge in 20 to 25 fathoms, preferably starting on a low slack tide and continuing through the flood. Try to choose a day with mild tidal flows, because the water can move fast here on a big tide.

If the fish aren't hitting, you might try trolling – with downrigger – northwest along the east side of the bank toward Wilson. Try to troll with the tide, rather than against it. At Point Wilson, by the way, anglers do well at times on chinook from the beach. It's one of the few places in Western Washington where that's the case.

In late summer, a troller can do very well here on hooknose silvers.

You can launch at public ramps at Point Hudson, the Port of Port Townsend Boat Haven, Fort Flagler and Fort Worden state parks. All are free, and all have adequate parking.

* * *

Chapter Eight

Hood Canal

————◆————◆————◆————◆————◆————◆————

F EW PLACES ON EARTH ARE AS LOVELY AS
Hood Canal on a soft, summer day. This is not a canal
in the classic sense, so don't let its name fool you. There's
nothing artificial about it.

This is a natural finger of Puget Sound, stretching south
and then east like a giant fishhook, from its entrance near
Foulweather Bluff to its end near Belfair, 80 miles away.
Stately Douglas firs press close to its gravel beaches, and the
Olympic Mountains tower in snowcapped magnificence over
its western shore.

Shellfish abound in the relatively warm waters here.
Hardshell clams can be had for the taking, and succulent oys-
ters litter the beaches. Dungeness crabs are easy to catch if
you know where to put your pots, and large spotted shrimp
draw tens of thousands of people here every spring for the
sport-shrimping season.

There was a time when this was a paradise for salmon anglers, too. But the canal started falling on hard times in the
late 1970s, when sport catches dropped off dramatically. The

Washington Fisheries Department says the reasons are complex. Local anglers attribute the decline to exploding populations of fish-eating marine mammals, and to increased competition from Indian and non-Indian commercial fishermen.

Despite the problems, Hood Canal can be worth a visit. Winter blackmouth fishing still can be good, and when mature ocean fish are migrating in, the results can be excellent if purse seiners and gillnetters give the sportsmen a chance.

The northern canal around Seabeck generally is the most productive, and this would be a good place for an angler to start. Salmon are easier to find here than in the south, and dogfish — a major problem in the south — are a little less so here.

A chinook angler will thrill to his first view of Seabeck. The canal widens out here, where Dabob Bay comes in from the northwest to join the main body of water, and points of land abound. Any experienced angler will recognize the opportunities.

Blackmouth are available from about mid-December to the end of March. A major blackmouth-producer is Hazel Point, on the Toandos Peninsula north of Seabeck, especially on an ebb tide, when nice eddies form just north of the point. Bait often gathers here, attracting feeding chinook. You can mooch here in close if the dogfish allow it, or you can troll all the way to Brown Point, north of Bangor. But remember: The Navy operates a submarine base at Bangor on the canal's eastern shore, and boaters have to stay on the opposite side.

Oak Head, at the southern end of the Toandos Peninsula, can be fished on either tide, and Tskutsko Point, northwest of Oak on the Dabob Bay side of the peninsula, is good on the flood.

On the eastern shore of the canal, right at the entrance to Seabeck Bay, is Misery Point. Misery sometimes will produce when the others won't.

Big Beef Creek and Little Beef Creek flow into Hood Canal a mile or two northeast of Seabeck, on the eastern shore, and anglers often take winter blackmouth off the mouth of each. South of Misery Point is Stavis Bay, and the entrance to it sometimes is good.

Trolling with hoochies or plugs is popular on the canal, mainly to discourage dogfish — which are a bigger problem the farther south you go. Many anglers use downriggers here, although some prefer meatlines.

Hood Canal, from one end to the other, is definitely an early morning fishery. But there's a twist to it. In much of the canal, you'll rarely find salmon near the surface at the first gray light of day the way you will in other areas. The water's warmer here, and that may be why you often need to go deeper here than you do elsewhere.

Blackmouth move around a lot here, and finding them one day doesn't mean you'll find them at the same place the next. You need to prospect each time, by looking for birds and bait, or for schooling fish on your depthsounder.

Ocean chinook begin to show in August, and will be in the area until mid-September. You fish for them the same way you do for winter blackmouth. Hazel is the place to begin, but don't overlook the mouths of the Big Beef and Little Beef, because some of the mature chinook run up those streams, too.

Ocean silvers start to show toward the end of August, and can provide a fishery through October. They like to school between Tskutsko Point and Hazel Point, and on the inside of Misery Point in Seabeck Bay. Try trolling cut-plug herring, or a flasher and a fly.

Chum, or dog salmon, arrive about October 1 in massive numbers, heading for virtually every little creek on the canal, and the fishery for them can continue until mid-December. Most effective are Buzz Bombs or erratic-acting lures such as Hot Shots and Tadpollys trolled from a downrigger about 70 feet deep. Greens and reds are favorites. You'll often find chum cruising in the deep water between Hazel and Seabeck Bay.

In odd-numbered years, pinks arrive about August 1, and continue to pass through until about the end of September. Many are headed for the Hamma Hamma and the

Dosewallips rivers, although a few go up the Big Beef. They sometimes school by the thousands in the shallows between Misery Point and Scenic Beach State Park, just to the southwest, and around the mouth of Pleasant Harbor, directly across the canal. They'll rarely take bait here, but they will go for erratic lures and Buzz Bombs. You'll be casting to them, mostly, because they're in such shallow water.

Fishing the southern canal is simpler in many ways, because the topography is less varied.

The dominant feature here is what anglers call the Great Bend, where the canal makes its fishhook turn to the east. The major landmark on the inside of the bend is Ayres Point, also called Bald Point, where most of the fishing occurs.

Winter blackmouth begin to show here between Thanksgiving and the second week of December. As in the north, early morning is by far the best, and direction and stage of tide don't seem to make much of a difference. Speed of the current does, however. The bite will be shorter on a strong tide, lasting as little as 30 minutes after first light. When tidal currents are slow, the fish might feed all morning.

Many local anglers troll at Bald Point, running a route from about a mile north of the point to about a mile-and-a-half east, near where the Tahuya River enters the canal. White-bodied Tomic or Silver Horde plugs work well in the 3-to 5-inch size. Troll near the bottom, close to the beach, along the 90- to 120-foot line.

Winter blackmouth fishing continues through February, then begins to taper off in March, when many of the fish apparently follow the bait into the northern canal. April through July is very slow, even in the best of years.

About the first week in August, ocean chinook start to arrive. They're headed for the state Fisheries Department hatchery at Hoodsport, a few miles northwest of Bald Point, and for the Skokomish River, which empties into the canal on the outside of the curve at the Great Bend. These fish will move in off Bald Point and, if rain is sparse, will stay there well into September. Many weigh into the 20s, and some scale into the 30s.

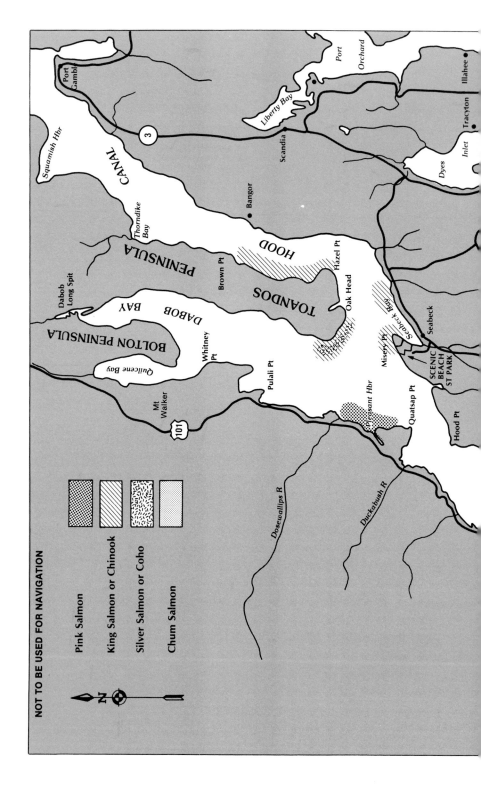

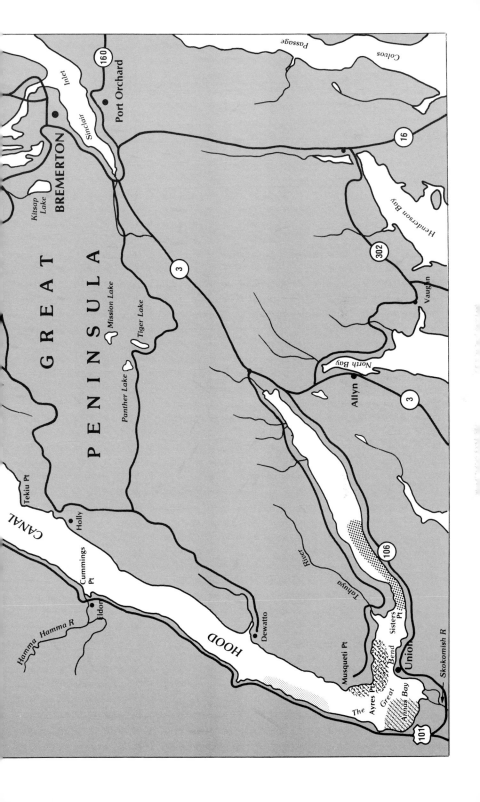

Local anglers catch them the same way they catch black-mouth, using downriggers to pull a plug or a flasher and hoochie.

When a lot of fish are in, you sometimes find them on the canal's south side, right off Alderbrook Inn, following the 90-foot line, and east of there in a place called the chicken hole.

Often, the kings will gather in Annas Bay, off the mouth of the Skokomish, just before going up the river, and you can take them there on Buzz Bombs. Watch for herring balls, watch for birds, and watch your depthfinder. Try to cast to the fish. Let the lure drop to the bottom before you start to jig it — a couple of feet at a stroke. Blue pearl and gray pearl, in the 4-inch model, are effective here.

Ocean coho start to arrive around Labor Day. They're headed for the Hoodsport hatchery, for the Skokomish River, for the Tahuya River, for the Union River at the canal's far end, and for Mission Creek, which crosses the northern beach a couple of miles west of Belfair. You must prospect for a school that's waiting to head upriver. Use a 4-inch Buzz Bomb — pink is good — and cast to them. They're usually easy to find, because they'll be jumping and rolling.

Sometimes they'll gather at the chicken hole to wait for rain, and you can find them there day after day. Or, they might gather off the north shore of the canal between Bald Point and Sisters Point.

The coho remain until precipitation calls them out of the saltchuck — usually the first good rain in October.

Chums are the last to arrive from the sea, bound for the Hoodsport hatchery and for the Skokomish. You can fish them in the canal itself, casting a 3-inch Buzz Bomb. A white one works well, especially if one side is painted a fluorescent color. In November, you can catch them in the Skokomish River. They're very aggressive, and will readily take a silver spinner.

Launching is easy on Hood Canal. In the north, the Marina and Moorage at Seabeck has a sling that can handle most boats to about 19 feet. A free Wildlife Department ramp with space to park about 25 vehicles and trailers is located nearby, on the west side of Misery Point. It has no float and no breakwater, however, and a strong south wind can make launching and retrieving impossible. The ramp also has little incline, and large boats – those of about 18 feet and longer – can be floated only a couple of hours either side of high slack tide.

On the west side of the canal is a pay ramp at the Triton Cove Trailer park, a few miles south of the Duckabush River. It is exposed to the weather, and too steep for some vehicles.

Another is located at Yelwick's General Store, a couple of miles north of Brinnon. It is exposed to the south, however, and may not be usable when the prevailing south wind is blowing hard.

Anglers may use a free ramp at the Fisheries Department shellfish laboratory at Point Whitney, although parking there is limited. Another ramp is located inside the Quilcene Boat Basin on the western shore of Quilcene Bay. It is the best protected of all, since it is located inside a breakwater, but it is farthest from much of the fishing.

On the southern canal, there's a free public ramp at Union, alongside Hood Canal Sports. Parking is limited, though, and requires leaving your rig on the highway's narrow shoulder. On a low tide, beware of the mud flat that extends from Union around into Annas Bay. A boater returning on a direct course from Bald Point may run aground.

Another public ramp with adequate parking is located at Potlatch, a few miles west of Union, and another is located at Twanoh State Park on the canal's south side a few miles west of Belfair.

* * *

Chapter Nine

The San Juans

IF I WERE TO DESIGN MY OWN VERSION OF paradise, it would look a lot like the San Juans in summer – rocky, fir-covered islands in a placid sea, hiding hundreds of little harbors and coves. Bald eagles wheel overhead, and hungry fish abound.

On many of the islands are state marine parks, where you can anchor, tie up to a buoy or moor to a float and go ashore, if you like, to pitch a tent under the trees. Picnic tables, fire rings and pit toilets are provided, and sometimes piped-in water.

You have found such a place, at the end of a day's fishing. As the dusk thickens you throw some more wood on the fire, then scrape together some coals and set fresh salmon steaks on a grill to broil. Your companions sit by the flames, sharing laughter over the day's events. You look out beyond the flickering light to where your boat is riding on its tether in the deepening darkness. It's magic – a moment frozen in time. Life seems full and complete, and you want to be right where you are, doing just what you're doing, more than anything else in the world.

Nobody, if he can help it, goes to the San Juans only once. The place gets under your skin, calls you back again and again. But its beauty is only a part of its lure. The fishing alone makes a visit worthwhile. Rockfish and lingcod prowl its underwater pinnacles. Coho and pink and chinook salmon hunt herring in its tidal rips and off its rocky points.

The San Juans cover a lot of territory. There are scores of islands, hundreds of bays and coves, thousands of points and dropoffs and rips. Everywhere you look you see salmon-angling potential. And any of these places may produce. Follow your instincts – explore, experiment and enjoy.

Over the years, however, some of these places have attained, in the lore of the sport, the stature of consistent producers, spots known for giving up certain kinds of fish at certain seasons.

If you're going to fish the San Juans, you have a major decision to make early on. You can launch near Anacortes, and run out from there, or you can ferry into the islands with your trailered boat behind your rig, and set up camp at a marine park or at a resort.

If you launch near Anacortes, your best bet is Washington Park, a modern and efficient place run by the city. It has a two-lane ramp, with floats, and provides adequate parking in an area that's patrolled. There's a fee to launch and to retrieve. You put your money in a box, and a barrier lifts out of your way.

Towing your boat onto a Washington State Ferry can be expensive. But it means you'll be able to return to the mainland whenever you want. Much of the water in the San Juans is quite well protected. But the return to Anacortes, across Rosario Strait, can be tricky if the wind is howling out of the north or the south.

Launch ramps are located on all of the islands with ferry service. Some are free, some have a fee. Local residents can direct you to them.

Blackmouth start showing in October, and one of the better spots for them then is off Cattle Point, on the southeast

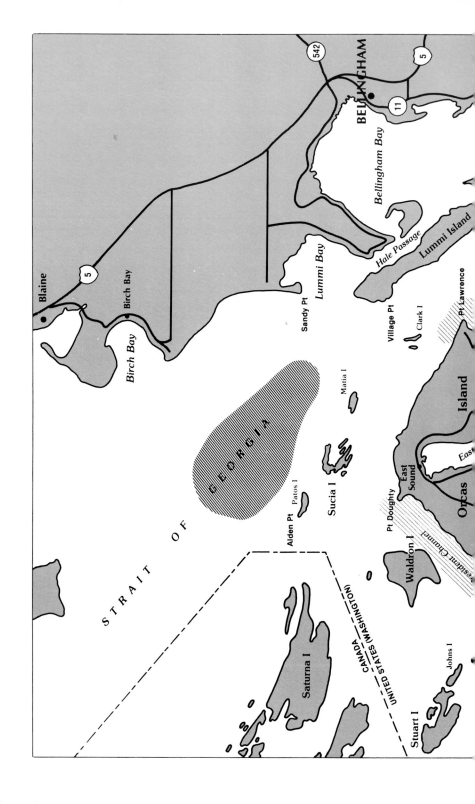

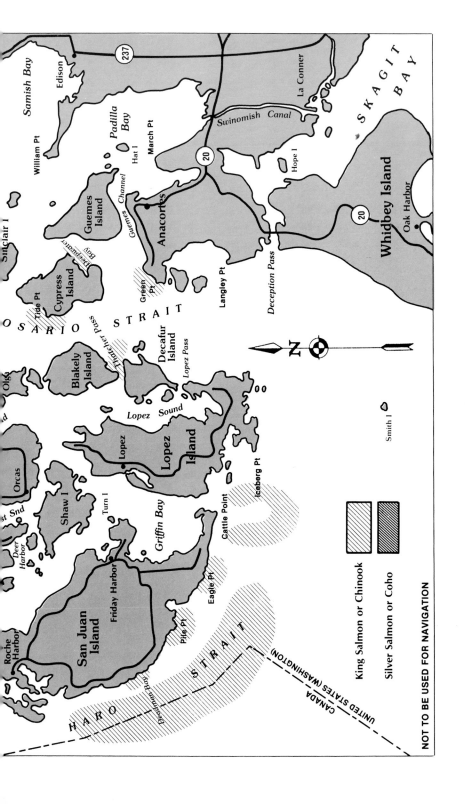

NOT TO BE USED FOR NAVIGATION

King Salmon or Chinook

Silver Salmon or Coho

corner of San Juan Island, the namesake of the group. Point Lawrence, on the eastern tip of Orcas Island, can begin to produce about this time, and so can Tide Point, about two-thirds of the way up the western side of Cypress Island.

The fishing improves elsewhere in November, and Thanksgiving through February is prime time for black-mouth everywhere in the islands. The area's a mixing place for fish from all directions. They come down from Canada, up from Oregon and in from the Washington coast. Even now it can be spotty, though – good one week, poor the next, then good again.

If you happen to be launching at Anacortes, stop first at Green Point, right near the ramp at Washington Park, then stop again directly across Rosario Strait in Thatcher Pass.

Throughout the winter, one of the more productive places is the west side of Orcas, from Deer Harbor to Point Doughty. Troll in close here, with a downrigger and cut-plug herring, following the 80- to 120-foot line just off the beach.

Blackmouth can be anywhere, but they do move around in the San Juans, and sometimes you have to hunt them down. When you find them, it's generally worth the effort, though. They run mostly 7 to 10 pounds now, with some into the high teens and the 20s, and every winter a few topping 30 pounds are brought to the boat.

About March, the fishing drops off temporarily, then sometime in April turns again for the better. Spring fish are beginning to show now, running mostly 12 to 20 pounds, and Point Lawrence is a prime place to take them. Tide Point, on Cypress, is good once again, and so is Cattle Point on San Juan Island. Deepwater Bay, on the southeast side of Cypress, can be good at this time, although it's even better in the summer.

Both moochers and trollers fish Lawrence on the ebb, catching the rip off the point and riding it south. Occasionally, trollers will connect off the north shore, north of the point, when the tide is inbound. They may pull a flasher and hoochie, or a plug.

When you're fishing the ebb, put your gear right on the bottom, in 80 to 140 feet, depending on where you think the fish will be. A lot of moochers fish Canadian-style here, with 10 1/2-foot rods and a half-pound of lead, backing down against the current, if necessary, to keep their line vertical.

About June, large fall-run chinook start showing consistently on the west side of San Juan Island. Eagle, Pile and Lime Kiln points are good places to look. You don't have to fish very far from the beach. You can mooch or dawdle along with a downrigger and cut-plug. Look for a rip off a point, and get into the back eddy nearby where a chinook might go to get out of the current. Pile Point is particularly good on the ebb, and Eagle also casts a nice shadow when the current moves south and east.

President Channel along the west side of Orcas can be good now, too.

Those old standbys, Tide Point and Lawrence, are churning out fish this time of year. So is Fishery Point on the northwest corner of Waldron Island.

A prime jig fishery also develops in early summer at Deepwater Bay. There are too many dogfish here that clamp onto mooched baits, so some anglers troll. But most of them turn to Buzz Bombs or Point Wilson Darts. When fishing gets hot, upwards of fifty boats may be crowding the spot.

A big, sandy shoal marks the bay's outer edge. Candlefish get up on the shoal, and chinook go up after them. An evening flood tide gives good fishing here, although you can fish on the ebb. High slack, if it's late in the day, is the best time of all.

You can find resident coho in the San Juans most of the year. They tend to stick to the southern part of Georgia Strait, north of Patos and Sucia islands, and around Alden Bank. By the end of June, they're running maybe 3 pounds apiece, and by the end of summer they'll average 6 to 7.

Ocean coho start to show in early August, and the western side of San Juan Island is the first place to look. By the end of August, the fishery really gets good, and it will stay that way through September. Find a nice tide rip out in Haro Strait, off one of the points that you fished for chinook, and you'll probably get some action there. Like chinook, coho also like to move up President Channel between Waldron and Orcas, and by the end of August that area can produce good fishing, too.

Sometimes you can catch coho on top, the way you do most other places, with a cut-plug herring or a strip, trolled 20 or 30 feet behind the boat. At other times, especially on the outside of San Juan Island, they're a little harder to please. If you don't find them on top, slow your troll a little and add some weight. Look for them at 60, 70 or 80 feet below the surface. If you have a downrigger, so much the better. Just fish your cut-plug right off that.

You'll usually find plenty of action, especially in September, because a couple of hundred thousand of these fish are passing through to Bellingham Bay. Additional thousands are headed for the Fraser River, at Vancouver, B. C., and for other Canadian tributaries on Georgia Strait.

In odd-numbered years, pink salmon fishing starts about the end of July, and improves as summer progresses. These 5-or 6-pound fish are headed mostly for the Fraser, and you'll find pinks in Haro Strait on the west side of San Juan, in Boundary Pass north of Waldron, in President Channel next to Orcas, and even a few in Rosario Strait, off Anacortes, although that's not a hot spot. The best place to catch them is off the west side of San Juan, fairly close to the beach. You won't have too much trouble finding them if they're around, because they'll be jumping. Keep your eyes peeled.

Mooching or motor-mooching will work, but the most effective way to catch pinks is with a dodger and a small hoochie in pink, orange or red.

* * *

Chapter Ten

North Sound

━━━━━━━━━━━━━━━━━━━━━━━━━

IF YOU HAVE TROUBLE CATCHING SALMON, you're going to love the North Sound — at least in odd-numbered years.

That's when pink salmon return by the hundreds of thousands, most bound for the Stillaguamish and Snohomish rivers, with a few headed for the Skagit. They fill the Snohomish, and anglers fill the water in front of the river, from Everett all the way to Mukilteo.

It starts in late summer, and it's wild and exciting, both on the water and at the ramps. At the six-lane ramp in Everett, for instance, anglers will be coming back in with their limits before others in line have even been out.

Pinks are easy to catch, and one way to do it is with a fire-red, 3-inch Red Magic spoon. Even better is a white No. 0 or No. 1 dodger pulling a squid or a mini squid.

Size of the squid may be optional, but color is not. The squid must be pink or red. Some of those who do best use a translucent, hot-pink model, and they fish it very slowly. They don't even turn the dodger — just let it swing back and forth. They fish right off the river, in 80 to 90 feet of water, sometimes right up into its mouth.

There's a lot more to North Sound than pinks, though. And there's a whole different feel to the fishing. You'll find it by running southwest, leaving Everett awash in your wake. There, a dozen miles from the city's smoky stacks, the melancholy sound of a bell buoy rolls out to greet you, coming across the water like a layer of oil, the way a train whistle wails across the empty reaches of the high plains.

There's a haunting quality to the sound, especially on a gentle day when the buoy rolls easily in the swells, clanging with a measured, funereal beat. It's a sound you'll come to know well if you fish Possession Bar.

But the sound is all that's melancholy at Possession. Because for much of the year this vast underwater reef at the southern end of Whidbey Island is a gathering place for salmon from all over Puget Sound, and anglers flock here from miles away to take part in some of the finest and most enjoyable fishing to be had anywhere east of the Pacific Ocean.

They come in large numbers, because Possession's location between Everett and Seattle puts it within easy range of the major population centers of Washington, which happens to be – after California – the most densely populated of all the western states.

The fish that move through here are headed from the ocean to a variety of places; some are southbound for the Green River or the Lake Washington system in central Puget Sound, others for the Puyallup River system near Tacoma, and others are on their way to Minter Creek, Chambers Creek, the Nisqually River or other locations in southern Puget Sound. Still others round the corner at Possession and go north, through Possession Sound to spawning areas on the Snohomish or the Stillaguamish river systems. Some turn the corner and then bear left up Saratoga Passage, all the way to the Skagit, preferring to round Possession Point rather than go straight across the northern end of Whidbey through Deception Pass.

The bar itself extends as much as 1 1/2 miles south from the southern end of Whidbey Island, lying between Possession Point on the east and Scatchet Head on the west.

As good as the fishing here can be, however, it's not a year-around thing. January through March, the bait fish go elsewhere, and the salmon follow. About April, the herring return, and the blackmouth come with them, like wolves with the caribou. By the middle of April, big spring chinook are arriving, and April through June can provide some of the finest fishing of the entire year. Fish are thick here now, and their size is probably as large, on the average, as you will find at any other time.

July starts off a little slower, but that turns out to be just a valley between the peaks. By the end of July, the first fall chinook are starting to arrive from the ocean in a run that will peak around the end of the first week in August.

Ocean silvers start to show as early as July, but typically don't arrive in any real numbers until about the last week in August.

Most years, excellent silver fishing continues through September, depending on the commercial fishery and the weather. Too much gillnetting can really take the bloom off the sport fishery, though, and too much rain can send the silvers directly up the rivers.

By October the blackmouth fishery has resumed, and usually is excellent until about the first of the year. Blackmouth commonly tip the scale in the teens, and sometimes surpass 20 pounds. Not only is the fishing good, but you'll find the waters here a lot less crowded in the fall, when many sportsmen are off hunting and others simply are waiting for spring.

Chum salmon runs vary from year to year, and chums never make up a very large part of the sport catch. But they're usually available at Possession from mid-October through about Thanksgiving, and hooking a bright chum salmon is like tying into a Budweiser Clydesdale. Plan on watching a chum strip a lot of line from your reel.

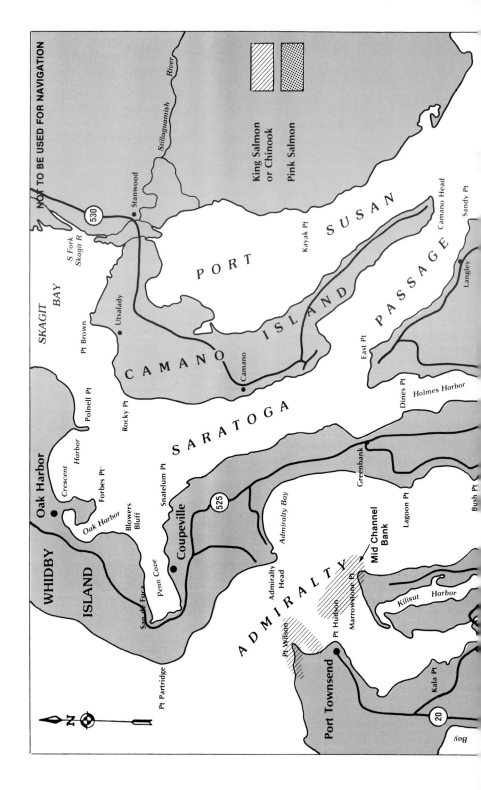

NOT TO BE USED FOR NAVIGATION

King Salmon or Chinook

Pink Salmon

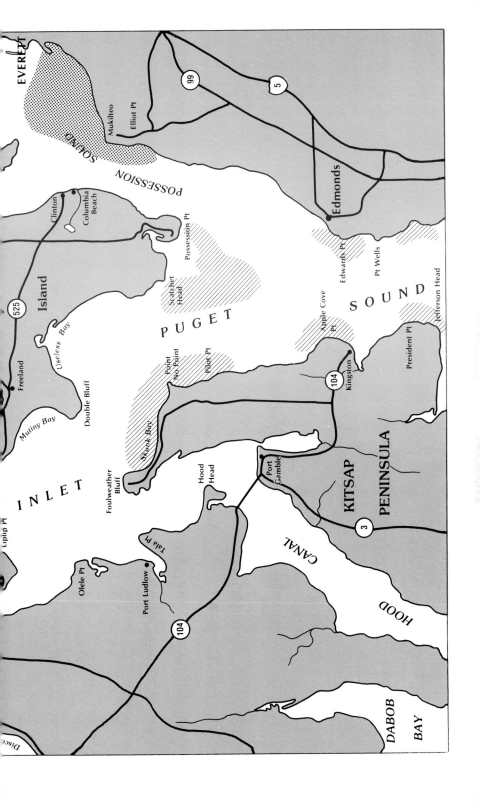

You can choose any style of fishing you prefer at Possession Bar. Some anglers mooch, and some even jig with Point Wilson Darts for chinook or Buzz Bombs for coho. But there's a whole lot of water to cover here, so most anglers troll with downriggers for chinook, either with plugs or with flasher and hoochie.

You should check the tide, then head for the lee side of the bar. Try to fish along its edges at 90 to 200 feet, exploring until you find the depth at which the fish are feeding.

Silvers, of course, are a different story. They have no affinity for bottom structure, and may be up against the kelp one day and out in the shipping lanes the next. You fish for them here the way you do in the Strait of Juan de Fuca. You get out in the rips and look for birds. When you find the birds you'll probably find the fish.

How do you get to Possession Bar? That's a problem. You can launch at several places on the mainland, including Seattle, and run north or south. It's a long run north from Seattle, though, about 15 miles from Shilshole Bay. And the wind is usually blowing out of the south, making for an even longer run back.

You can use the sling at the Port of Edmonds, cutting the run by more than half.

Closest to Possession is Mukilteo, which has a state park ramp, usually equipped with a small float from May through Labor Day. But the ramp is exposed to wind and waves, making it a difficult and sometimes dangerous place to launch and retrieve.

Farther north is Everett, where the excellent Port of Everett ramp on West Marine View Drive can be used for a modest fee. The ramp is in the Snohomish River, protected from the elements, and will handle as many as six boats at a time. However, Possession Bar is more than a dozen miles to the south.

Across Puget Sound, west of Possession Point, lies Point No Point on the northern end of the Kitsap Peninsula. Angling here can be as good as at Possession, and sometimes better.

Anglers do well at No Point at the start of the year, finding winter blackmouth from 4 to 10 pounds, with a few into the teens, January through March. But that's not the only thing that makes it different from Possession. Most of the people here are moochers, and they seem to do best near bottom in 100 to 150 feet of water. In winter, in fact, the fish seem to be closer to the bottom than at any other time.

As at Possession, the tide determines where you will fish, although it's not as important here in winter as it is the rest of the year. You might find fish right off the point or, in winter, straight out in front of the town of Hansville, just north of the point.

Another good area, just south of Point No Point, is known as "the flats." It's a shallows that extends out from the beach, deepening very gradually to about 100 feet. To fish it, you get out on the edge, where it starts to drop off, and put your cutplug herring near bottom in 120 to 150 feet. You can fish the flats on either tide.

In April and May, a few spring chinook begin to show. Resident coho, about a pound apiece, also are here now, but most anglers ignore them. May sometimes can provide very good fishing for spring chinook, but there's no guarantee.

About this time, the last couple of hours of an ebb becomes a good time to fish, and that will hold true through the summer. Many anglers gravitate now toward the eddy that's right off the light at the tip of the point.

In June, July and August, mature kings are rounding Point No Point, with the peak of the run passing through from about mid-July to mid-August. The last two hours of the ebb definitely are best now, and the first hour of the flood.

Time of day is less important than stage of the tide, but a midmorning or late-morning low seems to be best of all. A good bite also may develop right around high slack, especially if it occurs in the evening.

South of the point on the flats, you often find fish on the last couple of hours of the flood and at high slack.

When the silvers show in the first part of September, you can take them by mooching right off the point, as though you were fishing for kings. They seem to favor deeper water here than in most places, and you should be fishing 60 to 80 feet deep. If that fails, you can troll out in the rips, just as you would anywhere else.

For silvers, early morning is best, no matter what the stage of the tide, although lesser bites generally occur on high and low slacks, as well.

Kings usually are gone by the end of the third week of August, and silvers provide good fishing until about the middle of October. In November and December Point No Point will produce blackmouth again, and tides are not quite as important now as they were.

Some years, the chums bite fairly well here sometime between late October and the end of November. It will last only a week or so, and seems to be best from about an hour before low slack to about an hour after.

As it is on the other side of the sound, launching here can be a problem. The Point No Point Beach Resort at Hansville has a railroad launch that will accommodate boats to 16 feet. It takes the craft from its trailer by sling, deposits it on a rail car and rolls it into the water.

The Forbes Landing Resort nearby will accommodate some boats to 17 or 18 feet. Longer boats have to launch at Kingston, which is several miles south, or at the Hood Canal Bridge on the opposite side of the Kitsap Peninsula. The bridge launch can be tricky, because to reach Point No Point from there, a boat must round Foulweather Bluff, which is appropriately named.

An angler who has been fishing at the point could find a strong south wind roaring up Hood Canal, meeting him head-on as he rounds the bluff on his return. A wind from the north could be even worse, because it will hit the bluff before it reaches Point No Point. An angler trying to round the bluff to get back to the ramp could find waves stacking up there.

* * *

Chapter Eleven

Seattle and Central Puget Sound

————————————————————

I N A WAY, CENTRAL PUGET SOUND IS A BEACON of hope for people who love the Pacific salmon. It provides a peek into the future, and the scenario it reveals is encouraging. It shows a sophisticated, urban environment and – right along with it – a glimpse of nature at its most enthralling.

It's immediately apparent to anyone who is on the water here with rod in hand. To the east, Seattle's high-rise skyline towers above the traffic, its futuristic Space Needle putting a Northwest stamp on the scene. Around your boat, super ferries, grain ships and container ships ply Elliott Bay, churning up wakes in the slate-gray water. Above the boat, jumbo jets hang low in the sky, flaps down, lining up with runways at Seattle-Tacoma International Airport.

But that isn't all. Below the boat, just out of sight of this urban anthill, schools of sockeye, coho and chinook salmon respond to the same elemental forces that have driven them for eons. They swarm back to their rivers of origin in this busy inland sea.

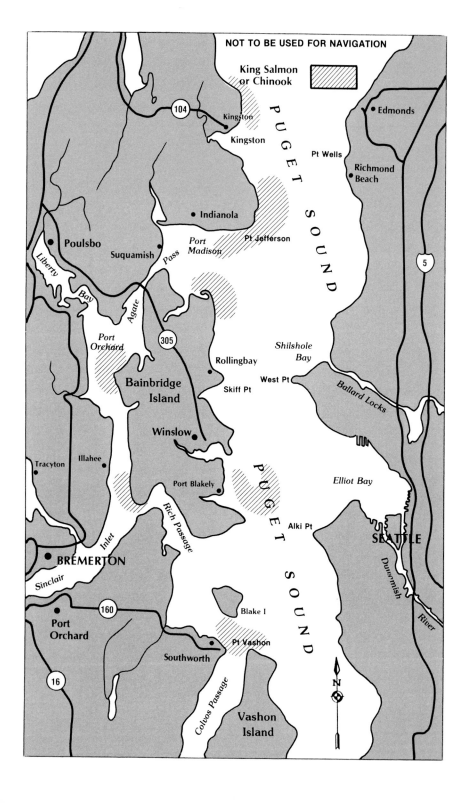

It's a thrilling thing to experience, this meeting of the old and the new. It offers some promise that if we place a high enough value on the fish, if we pay enough attention to their needs, they may prove to be at least somewhat tolerant of the changes we have wrought in their environment.

Fishing is at its best here in the summer and the fall, when ocean-grown fish are returning as adults. But year-round angling is available, with blackmouth making up the winter catch.

For anglers launching in Seattle, this often means a cross-Sound run, because some of the best winter fishing is outside of Elliott Bay. Blake Island is a good place to start. It is southwest of West Seattle's Alki Point and northwest of the northernmost point of Vashon Island. Troll a triangle from the southern tip of Blake to the northern tip of Vashon, then southwest to the ferry dock at Southworth on the Kitsap Peninsula, and back to Blake. If that does not produce, you can troll between Southworth and Manchester, on a southeast-northwest line to the west of Blake Island. A flasher and hoochie, fished off a downrigger, can be very effective here.

North of Blake Island, past Restoration Point on the southeast tip of Bainbridge Island, is Blakely Rock. It lies off the entrance to Bainbridge's Blakely Harbor, and is another good place for winter blackmouth, which feed among the nearby tidal rips.

Off the northern end of Bainbridge Island, across Port Madison, lies Jefferson Head, a popular blackmouth area on the northern Kitsap Peninsula. Early morning fishing can be excellent here, especially on a tide change and on the ebb.

These fisheries all peak between February and May, when spawning herring school around Blake and Bainbridge islands, and at Jefferson Head.

North of Jefferson on the Kitsap Peninsula is a place called Apple Cove Point. It often produces nice blackmouth.

Directly across Puget Sound from Jefferson Head, on the mainland north of Seattle, is an area just north of Carkeek Park called The Trees. The trees themselves have long since been cut down, but a black can buoy marks the spot where three big cottonwoods grew along an old railroad right-of-way, and it provides good spring and summer fishing for kings. You can mooch here or you can troll, with the 100- to 120-foot depths generally the most productive.

North of the trees on the mainland side of the Sound opposite Apple Cove Point is Edmonds. It can provide some excellent blackmouth fishing November through January. February and March can be hot or cold. You generally find either good fishing then or none at all.

The fishing is very concentrated here in winter, and most of it takes place right in front of the Edmonds oil tanks. Fish in 90 to 200 feet of water, making a circle in front of the tanks.

Tomic plugs are popular here. So are Apex lures, which are plastic spoons with a bend in the forward end. Fish either lure 30 to 60 feet behind a downrigger.

Point Monroe, on the northeast tip of Bainbridge Island, can be every bit as good as Jefferson Head. Fish it the way you would Jeff, on the ebb through low slack.

As you make the turn around the northern end of Bainbridge Island, you enter Agate Pass, perhaps best known for its Pacific cod fishery in February. What's not as well known is that some nice blackmouth feed here in the spring, and they'll hammer a trolled lure or a flasher and hoochie.

Just north of Agate Pass on the Kitsap Peninsula is Miller Bay. A sport fishery develops in July and August right off its mouth for chinook reared there by the Suquamish Indian Tribe.

About a third of the way down the west side of Bainbridge Island is Battle Point, where a good spring blackmouth fishery often can be found. South of there on the southwest tip of Bainbridge is Point White. Waters south of White can provide very good winter and spring fishing for chinook. Troll deep – 120 to 130 feet.

About May, resident coho sometimes start to school in Elliott Bay, off Duwamish Head. Then, about the middle of June, big kings start moving in, a few weighing 30 pounds or more. Anglers begin picking them up off West Seattle between Alki Point and Duwamish Head. That fishery gradually works its way into the inner bay, peaking there about the Fourth of July.

With the middle of July comes another run of kings. And from then into September, kings will be coming through fairly steadily, headed up the Duwamish Waterway into the Green River.

You should fish along the beach, trolling a plug or a hoochie or a cut-plug herring along the 120-foot line, working your way farther and farther into the bay as the summer gets older. By late in the season, if regulations allow it, you should be fishing right off the river mouth.

Meanwhile, another run of kings is moving in just north of Elliott Bay. It's the Lake Washington run, which comes in across the Ballard Flats, through the Hiram M. Chittenden Locks and the Lake Washington Ship Canal into Lake Union, then moves from there to Lake Washington and beyond. It will begin to show about the first week of June, and will continue to come through into September. The best way to take these fish is on the flats, just outside the Canal, with trolled herring and a few ounces of lead.

It's nice to have help when you get a big one to the boat.

93

Sockeye returning to the Cedar River move through the Ship Canal and into Lake Washington in early summer, with run size peaking at the locks about the Fourth of July. If the size of the run permits, the state Fisheries Department allows a sport fishery on sockeye in Lake Washington, where anglers slow-troll U-20 Flatfish in shades of red, or bare blue Gamakatsu hooks. Lures or bare hooks are pulled behind a flasher or dodger. Silvers start to show about the last week of August. You'll generally find them first well out in the Sound, and anglers will run out to fish for them offshore. As the fish work their way into Elliott Bay, the anglers follow, trolling near the surface, sometimes with just herring and 3 or 4 ounces of lead. These fish stay away from the beach, even after they've moved into the bay, and you have to be alert to where you are and what's going on around you, because ferry and freighter traffic can be heavy here at times.

Depending on commercial fishing pressure, these silvers may continue to show in good numbers well into October.

Spring usually is the best time to fish Blake Island, but a fair number of silvers show here, too, in the fall. The old triangle, from the south tip of Blake to Vashon to the Southworth ferry dock can be productive. Look for birds working the water, and fish where they do.

Restoration Point, at the south tip of Bainbridge Island, can be good for silvers in the fall, and so can Blakely Rock above that. Yeomalt Point, about halfway up the island on its eastern side, can produce from time to time, and it's worth a check if you're in the neighborhood.

Seattle has numerous launch ramps on Lake Washington, which lies along the city's eastern boundary, but an angler launching there has to travel through the locks to get to Puget Sound. On a beautiful summer weekend that can mean a delay of hours as traffic backs up.

Launching in the Sound makes more sense, but facilities are fewer. One ramp is located in West Seattle, near Duwamish Head, and another near the Ship Canal, at the north end of Shilshole Bay Marina.

* * *

Chapter Twelve

Tacoma and South Puget Sound

I T WAS AS UNLIKELY A SALMON-ANGLING SCENE as you could imagine. Big smokestacks belched effluent into the late-summer sky from the sprawling Tacoma industrial area that lined both sides of the river. Just outside the river's mouth, grain ships and log ships rode at anchor in Commencement Bay, awaiting their turns to take on cargo bound for the other side of the Pacific. Burly tugboats plied the waters, towing barges and pushing ocean-going vessels into and out of crowded berths.

Around and through it all buzzed a mosquito fleet of tiny boats, 14-, 15-, 16-footers, some a little larger, weaving in and out among the commercial vessels and back and forth across the mouth of the Puyallup River.

The little boats were trolling for silver salmon, bright hooknose fish that were returning to the river from the sea. These fish arrive from late August through September, and anglers turn out in droves to intercept them near Brown's Point, where the silvers round the corner into the bay, and along the north side of the bay all the way to the Puyallup River itself.

Deep Sixes are particularly effective here, especially when pulling a fresh, plug-cut herring. A good place to use them is right off the mouth of the Puyallup, preferably on a flood tide, where the milky waters of the glacial river empty into the bay.

A nice chinook caught on a mooched herring by Terry Whitworth in waters near Port Angeles, Washington.

The fresh water, being lighter, rides atop the saltwater upon entering the bay. Let out about 15 pulls of line. That will be enough to take your bait down through the glacial silt and into the clear saltwater beneath it. And that's right where the fish will be.

You also can look for ocean silvers near Point Fosdick at the southwest entrance to the Tacoma Narrows, at the concrete dock on the southeastern side of Fox Island, and at Day Island which lies off the eastern shore of the Sound just south of the Narrows.

Farther south, look for hooknose silvers in September around Johnson Point and near the saltwater net pens at Squaxin Island. Gull Harbor, near the northern end of Budd Inlet, is another good place to check. A combination of wild stock and Squaxin stock mills there before making the final push home. Trolled flies, Buzz Bombs and Blue Fox French spinners all are popular coho- takers in South Puget Sound.

Tacoma-area fishing is more than just a late-summer thing, though. Winter blackmouth angling usually begins about Thanksgiving, and can continue strong through February and even March. Point Defiance can be productive on an ebb tide for anglers mooching right off the light or trolling a plug or a squid parallel to the claybanks in 15 to 30 fathoms. The Point can be mooched on a flood tide, as well, in the eddy inside the rip, right at the head of the Tacoma Narrows. That's where the fish are, up close to the light.

Point Evans on the northwestern shore of the Narrows is another good place to mooch in the winter. It's usually fished on the ebb or on a small flood. On the ebb, you drift from Evans north, 300 to 400 yards. On big tides, a large back eddy forms north of the point, where baitfish mill about. That's where the salmon will be. On smaller ebbs, the bait and the salmon stay farther from the beach, closer to the middle of the channel. On the small flood tides, you drift south, from the overhead power lines to the Narrows Bridge.

The entrance to Quartermaster Harbor, at the south end of Vashon Island, is a good winter blackmouth area. Anglers usually troll around the buoy at Quartermaster's entrance or back along the beach to the west of the buoy. Watch your

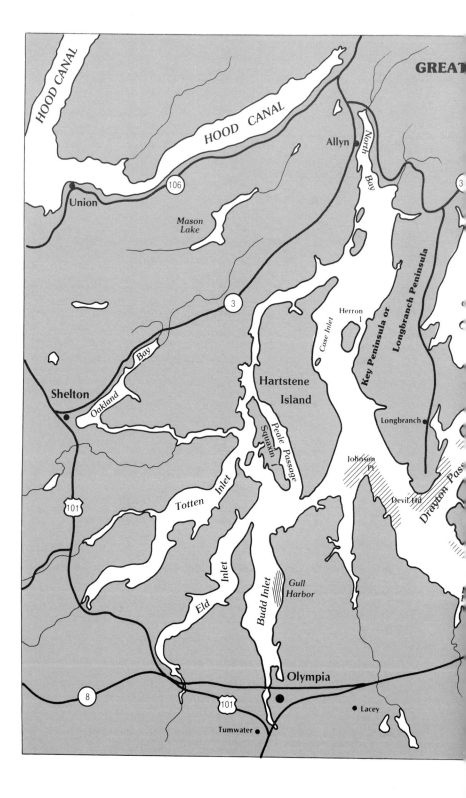

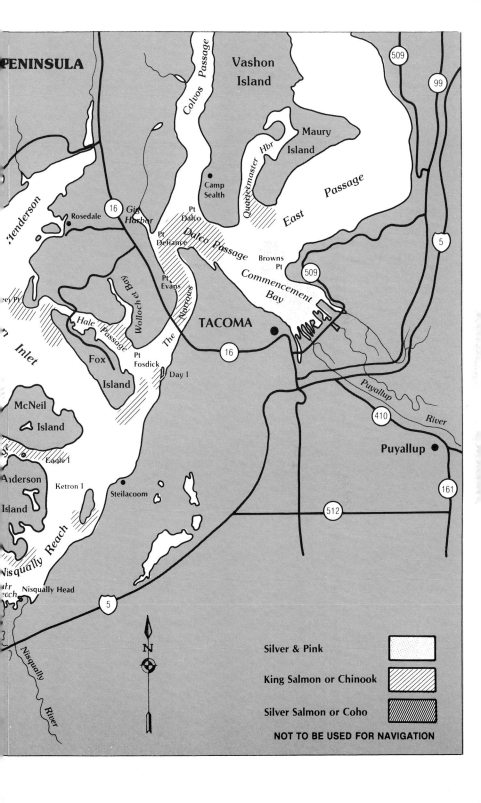

depthfinder, and stay in no less than 15 fathoms. The last of the flood tide and the first of the ebb generally are best there.

Point Dalco, just to the west of the harbor entrance, is traditionally a flood-tide fishery, usually best from low slack through the start of the flood. But it also can be fished on a small ebb. An angler can troll big figure-eights off the point, or he can move in close and troll right off the retaining wall. The bottom drops steeply here, and you should stay fairly close to the beach.

As popular as points Dalco and Defiance are in winter, they're even more productive from May through September. Migratory chinook like to gather in both places before making the final push to their rivers.

Point Fosdick, which produces silvers in September, can provide some good winter blackmouth fishing on the flood. A big back eddy forms just around the corner from the Narrows Bridge, and a lot of anglers find productive fishing here, especially on a big tide.

The Fox Island concrete dock is a popular winter blackmouth spot. It's usually fished on the ebb, but can be good on a small flood.

Farther south, winter blackmouth fishing can be productive at Eagle Island, at Ketron Island, off the south end of Anderson Island, at Johnson Point and at Devils Head. Tide changes are popular at Anderson, Johnson and Devils Head. Over the long run, it doesn't seem to matter whether it's high ebb or low ebb, although differences can be apparent from day to day.

Anderson generally is mooched. The most popular drift is from its southeast corner along the edges of the rip. On a flood tide, the area known as the staircase can be good. It's about a quarter-mile northwest of the southeast corner, and often produces blackmouth fairly close to the beach.

Blackmouth anglers like to troll the east side of Johnson Point in 10 to 13 fathoms, with downriggers, from about Zittel's Marina to the end of the point. Flasher-and-hoochie combinations are effective here, particularly with a herring strip on the trailing hook.

Johnson also can be mooched, and can be quite productive on the ebb, drifting from the point to the southeast.

Resident coho aren't usually very numerous in waters just north of the Narrows, but some years they provide a major fishery in waters to the south. Some anglers like to take them on cast flies in April and May in Hale Passage and along the eastern side of Johnson Point. Coho also gather off the south end of Anderson and at Devils Head, where small, trolled lures will take them.

About May, a few big ocean chinook begin to show at spots around Tacoma and the South Sound. Some of these are spring chinook, the remnant of a run from a Puyallup tributary that is headed for the Minter Creek Hatchery on Carr Inlet. Fall chinook show through June and July, gathering at the usual places – near the Point Defiance claybanks, at Point Dalco, and at Day Island, Point Fosdick and Anderson Island.

Day Island provides a good mooch fishery for big chinook in July and August. Look for a big flood tide – late afternoon usually is best – and drift south along Day Island's western side. You start on a shelf, in about 15 fathoms, and when you hit 35 or 40 fathoms you run back up and start another drift.

By August, chinook are piling up off the mouth of the Puyallup River and just outside the railroad trestle at the mouth of Chambers Creek. They're not feeding very actively now, and they can be hard to catch.

Launch facilities in the Tacoma area are good, although crowding can be a problem when the fishing is hot.

At Tacoma, boaters can take advantage of a modern, multilane public ramp at Point Defiance Park, for a minimal fee. A smaller, privately operated ramp is located at Narrows Marina at the south end of the Narrows. Free public ramps are located at Gig Harbor, in Wollochet Bay, at the Fox Island bridge, at Home and near Devils Head on the Longbranch Peninsula, and at Luhr Beach on the Nisqually Delta. Privately operated launching also is available on Johnson Point and at Boston Harbor on Budd Inlet. Avoid the municipal ramp at Steilacoom. Charges are high, and the facility is in poor condition.

Chapter Thirteen

Lower Columbia River and Washington Coast

‡·—·—·—·—·—·—·—·—·—·—·—·‡

IT'S A WONDERFUL, EXHILARATING, DANGEROUS fishery – thousands of boats crammed into the mouth of the mighty Columbia River, pitching and rolling in the slop, competing for space and for migrating ocean silvers and kings.

The name of the game is intimidation. Big boats bear down upon smaller ones in the strong tidal current, and skippers hurl warnings and challenges as line crosses line and whirling props threaten taut monofilament.

Ashore, it's nearly as crazy. Imagine police in the streets, directing traffic through town, so the thousands of rigs hauling boats to the ramp won't gridlock the city.

That's what happened in Ilwaco, Washington a few years ago as anglers flocked to the fishery known as Buoy 10. It takes place right inside the mouth of the Columbia, and is named for the numbered buoy that marks the seaward boundary of the area in which fishing occurs. About two million salmon enter the Columbia each year, but obviously the fishery isn't for everyone.

The water can be exceedingly rough when the wind rises here, and the south jetty area in particular can be treacherous with breaking waves. Usually the danger is visible, but a flood tide can push you right into it if you aren't alert, so it's a good idea to stay north of the red buoy line for safety.

How crowded does this river get? On the afternoon before one recent opening, traffic backed up from the launch ramp at Fort Canby State Park – an efficient, modern facility with good floats – literally for miles. Nearby, the sling launch at the Port of Ilwaco worked until midnight to accommodate anglers, then the operator returned at 3 a.m. to find a new line of trailered boats stretching into the darkness.

Both Canby and downtown Ilwaco are convenient to the fishery, which you reach through a channel behind Sand Island. But follow the channel markers, because it's easy to run aground here.

On the Oregon side, launch ramps are a longer run from Buoy 10. Astoria has one free ramp but it's hard to use on low tides. Better facilities are located just downstream at Warrenton, where a two-lane ramp is available at the Warrenton Boat Basin, about a mile from the Columbia on the Skipanon River. Hammond, even farther downstream, has a six-lane ramp right on the Columbia, but you still have about a seven-mile run to Buoy 10.

Don't expect to beat the Ilwaco crowds by launching in Oregon, though. During the height of the fishery, trailered boats will be lined up for several miles on the Oregon side as well. Hammond might launch 400 or 500 boats per day on a weekend, while Warrenton's smaller ramp might handle 80 or 100. If you plan to launch just once and then moor for a while, try to make your arrangements well in advance, because much of the moorage sells out ahead of time.

If you think fishing is about peace and solitude and gentle nourishment for the soul, Buoy 10 probably is not for you. But if you're confident with rough water and tough competition, this hotbed of salmon activity can provide an angling experience you'll never forget.

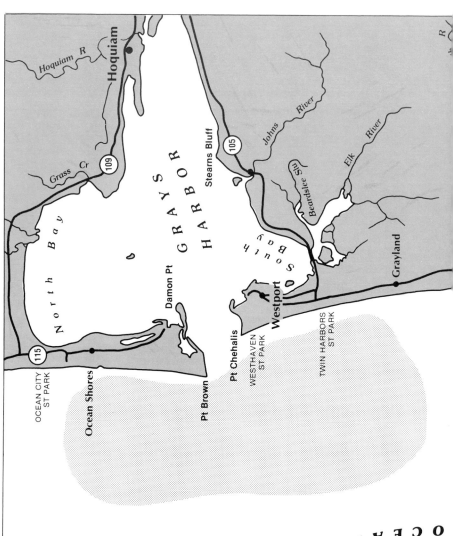

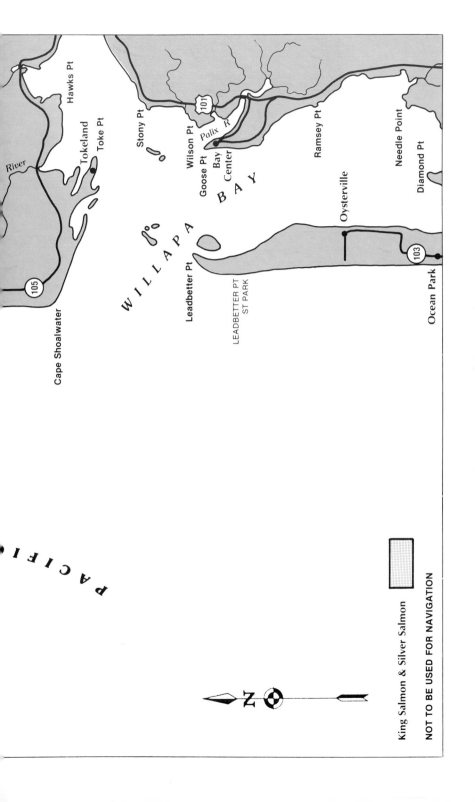

Hawks Pt

Tokeland
Toke Pt

River

Stony Pt

101

Wilson Pt
Palix R
Goose Pt
Bay
Center

Ramsey Pt

Needle Point

Diamond Pt

B A Y

Oysterville

Cape Shoalwater

105

W I L L A P A

Leadbetter Pt

LEADBETTER PT
ST PARK

103

Ocean Park

P A C I F I

N

King Salmon & Silver Salmon

NOT TO BE USED FOR NAVIGATION

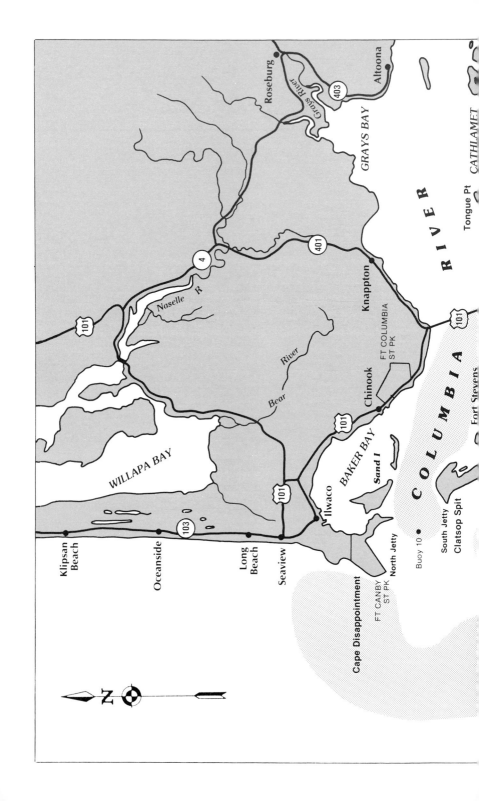

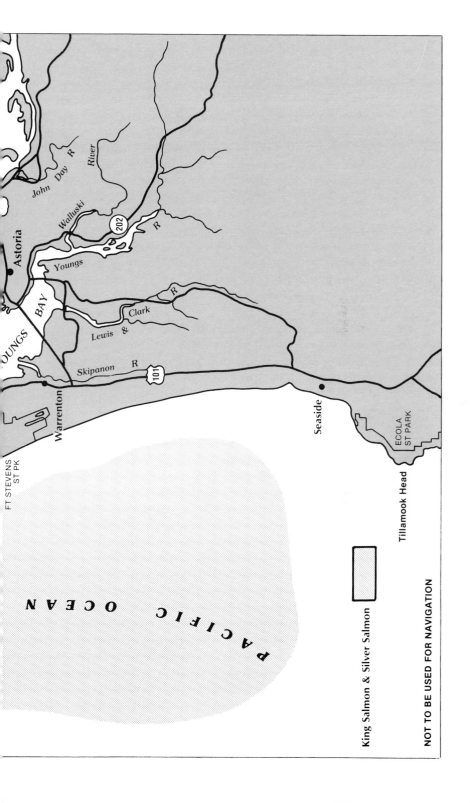

PACIFIC OCEAN

FT STEVENS
ST PK

Warrenton

Skipanon R

Astoria

YOUNGS BAY

Youngs

Walluski

John Day R

River

202

R

Lewis & Clark R

101

Seaside

ECOLA
ST PARK

Tillamook Head

King Salmon & Silver Salmon

NOT TO BE USED FOR NAVIGATION

Fall chinook hit the river about the middle of August. These are primarily Tules, headed for hatcheries on the lower Columbia. Coho usually are mixed among them, and fishing can be good well into September.

Use fresh bait — anchovies seem to be better than herring here — plug-cut or whole. Fish the incoming tide from low slack through high. You can find fish anywhere between Buoy 10 and Astoria, but many anglers like to push right into the crowd near Buoy 10, in the rips near where the river meets the ocean. Bait usually is plentiful here, and ocean fish may drift in and out with the tide many times, gorging on baitfish before finally heading upriver for good.

The water usually is no more than 60 feet deep, an ideal place for planers. Start with about 10 pulls of line, then strip out some more if you don't find fish quickly. Point your bow toward the ocean and troll against the incoming current, letting the tide back you slowly upriver.

When ocean fishing is open, small boats from Ilwaco and the Oregon river ports generally turn south beyond the bar and fish along the Oregon coast, because the area just to the north, in Washington, often is closed for conservation.

Anglers interested in fishing the Washington coast basically have only one choice, aside from Neah Bay, and that is Westport. La Push, on the Quileute Indian Reservation between Westport and Neah Bay, once was popular with small-boat anglers. But it has fallen out of favor because of tensions that arose there in the wake of federal court decisions on Indian fishing rights.

At Westport, your whole focus must be the formidable bar. You will want to cross it on a flood tide, although you can cross on an ebb if the ocean is flat. With any swell at all, however, the ebbing tide running against the swell will create steep, often breaking, waves.

Even on the flood the bar can be unpredictable, depending on the direction of the swell. A cross-wave can put a lot of water over your gunwale if you're not watching out.

You should have a local chart and a good tidebook, and know how to use them. Sometimes you'll have a half-hour's grace on the tail end of the high, when the water over the bar remains slack. The worst time of all is three or four hours after the high – the period of maximum ebb – when the bar is the nastiest.

You'll see boats of many sizes on the ocean around here if the day is calm, but many knowledgeable locals are reluctant to attempt the bar in anything smaller than an 18-footer. Channel 13 is the local Citizens' Band radio channel. An angler in trouble can use it to call for assistance, and be fairly sure that someone will relay his message to the Coast Guard inside the harbor.

Trolling is a good way to introduce a youngster, like John Mottram, to the thrill of battling a nice one.

Once you've crossed the bar, you often can find good fishing right in front of it, particularly for bigger chinook during afternoon tides. Often an angler will turn north or south, because the middle waters tend to remain fairly rough for two or three hours after the ebb.

The north beach off Ocean Shores is a productive place for chinook. Fish along the 10-fathom line, but be aware that with any swell at all the north spit can be very dangerous, because of the many commercial crab pots here. A lot of the heavy pots are buried immovably in the sandy ocean floor. Should you get a crab pot line wrapped around your prop, a large swell can pick you up and flip you like a piece of balsa. It's happened more than once, sometimes with tragic results.

A lot of anglers like to follow the red buoy line southwesterly. The first buoy in the line actually is yellow, and is marked with an SJ." It locates the end of a sunken jetty, and from there along the south beach is a prime area for larger fish. Again, 10 fathoms seems to be the magic number.

Beyond the SJ Buoy are buoys 8, 6, 4, 2 and finally the GH Buoy, which is about 3 miles from the harbor. It's a good idea for an angler who's inexperienced here always to keep a buoy in view, for help getting home if a fog comes down. Most small boats fish between the beach and the GH, and they catch both species of salmon here. The closer to shore you fish, the more likely you are to find bigger chinook. If you're targeting coho exclusively, you might consider running beyond the GH toward the six-mile line, which is at 25 fathoms. But remember, you're dealing with a big ocean.

Nearly all of the small-boat anglers here troll, rather than mooch, and a Deep Six or a Pink Lady is very effective, even for chinook. Sometimes, in fact, a big fish may hit while you actually can see the planer fishing just below the surface in only 20 or 30 feet of water.

Chinook always are feeding in the waters off Westport, but a major migration comes down the coast between mid-July and mid- August, and peaks in the Columbia River about the third week of August. Coho usually arrive from mid-June to early July, and also peak in the Columbia River in late August.

* * *

Chapter Fourteen

Oregon Coast

———————————————————————————

S ALMON ANGLERS HAVE A COUPLE OF wonderful things going for them in Oregon – excellent fishing, in the ocean and in the many coastal bays and one of the most beautiful coastlines in the world on which to enjoy it.

A wealth of angling opportunity exists here for small-boat fishermen, from the ports on the Columbia River just across the water boundary from Washington, to Brookings, near the California line.

Oregon anglers tend to troll almost exclusively, and they tend to favor planers – such as the Deep Six or the Pink Lady – over downriggers.

Columbia River

The northern end of the coast is dominated, of course, by the Columbia, which at its peak was probably the greatest salmon-producing river in the history of the world. It still produces its share, and anglers fish out of Columbia River ports all summer long.

When the ocean is open under state and Pacific Fishery Management Council regulations, many small-boat anglers cross the Columbia River bar, one of the most dangerous on the coast. Like all bars, it's usually worst on an ebbing tide, when boaters face the additional hazard of being swept out to sea if anything goes wrong. Each boat operator must decide for himself whether to attempt the crossing, depending on water conditions, weather, the seaworthiness of his boat, and his own ability as a skipper. Low slack and high slack usually provide the best bar conditions, with a flood tide the next-best time to try to cross. Sometimes the bar will be too rough even on an incoming tide, and the Coast Guard will close it to some or all recreational boats, and will announce the decision on Channel 16, VHF. It also will patrol the bar to turn back small craft.

An angler who does everything right can expect to have days like this. Not a bad catch for Terry Whitworth.

The entrance to the Columbia isn't always rough, but it is unpredictable. And you can't judge conditions by what you see where you launch. The day may be calm in the harbor, but when you get to the bar you may find it ugly. After crossing the bar, many boats turn south. Popular places are south of the south jetty and south of the red channel-marker buoys. Many boats will be fishing any day in the season that the weather permits, and newcomers can just follow them out.

Most chinook are caught within 3 miles of the beach, regulations permitting, although you may run several miles along the coast before you start fishing.

For coho, you may want to run out to the navigational buoy, then steer a southwesterly course of about 200 degrees. Troll for both species, a little deeper for chinook, with a fresh or frozen anchovy. Planers are popular for silvers, but rarely are used for chinook in this area. Most anglers here prefer 5 to 7 ounces of lead, and try to fish 20 to 30 feet below the surface.

Tillamook Bay

A few miles south on the Oregon coast is Tillamook Bay, fed by five rivers – the Miami, Kilchis, Wilson, Trask and Tillamook. All support salmon. The Wilson and Trask are the biggest, and by far the most productive.

Spring chinook start funneling into the bay about Mother's Day, headed mostly for the Trask. Coho become fairly numerous the middle of June, and stay that way through Labor Day, and fall chinook start to show late in July or the first part of August. Both species are bound for all five rivers. Many of the fall chinook are very large, and each season fish to 60 pounds or more are caught.

Anglers here fish both species in the ocean all summer, then fish for chinook in the bay starting about Labor Day. The in-bay fishery for coho is not as extensive as the one for chinook, apparently because anglers prefer to target the larger species, and because coho don't bite quite as well as chinook in the bay.

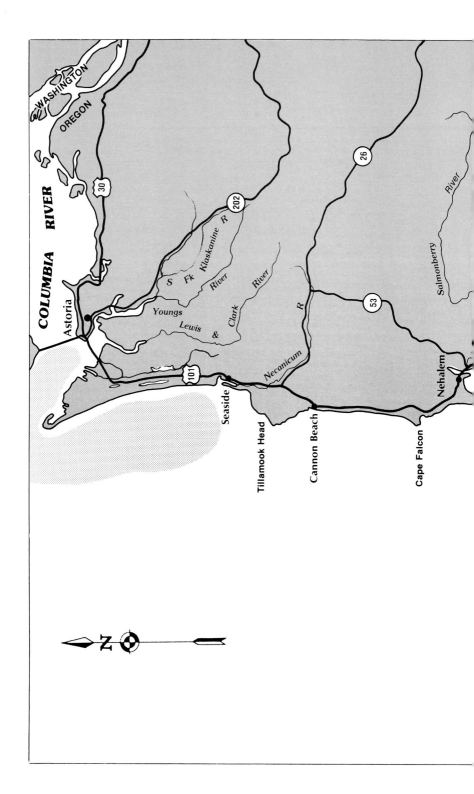

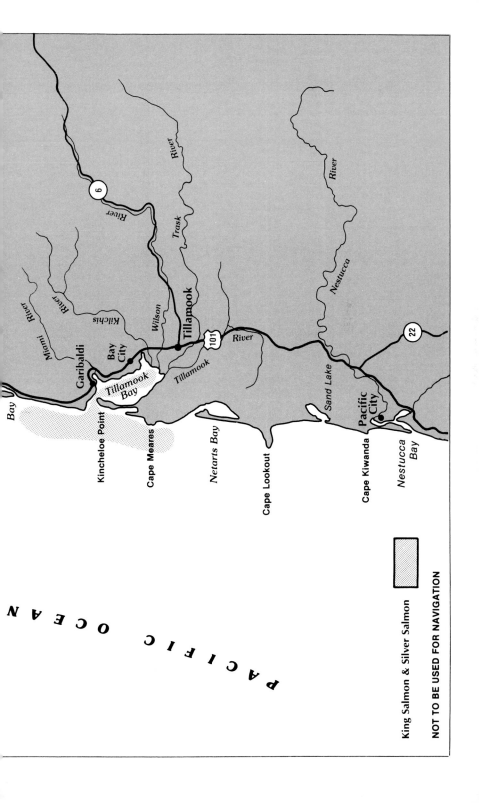

PACIFIC OCEAN

King Salmon & Silver Salmon

NOT TO BE USED FOR NAVIGATION

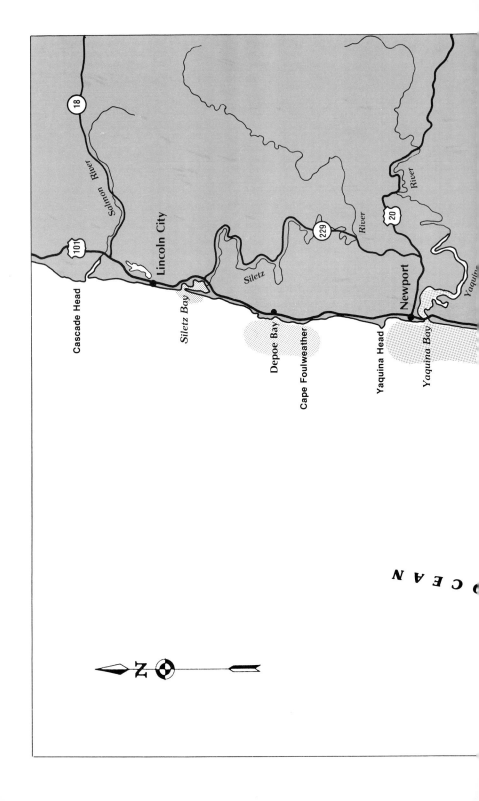

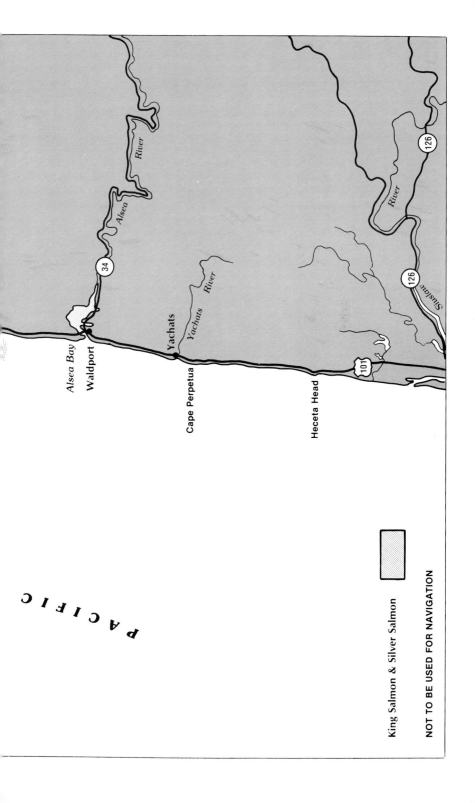

PACIFIC

Alsea Bay
Waldport

Alsea River

Alsea River

34

Yachats

Yachats River

Cape Perpetua

Heceta Head

101

126

Siuslaw

River

126

King Salmon & Silver Salmon

NOT TO BE USED FOR NAVIGATION

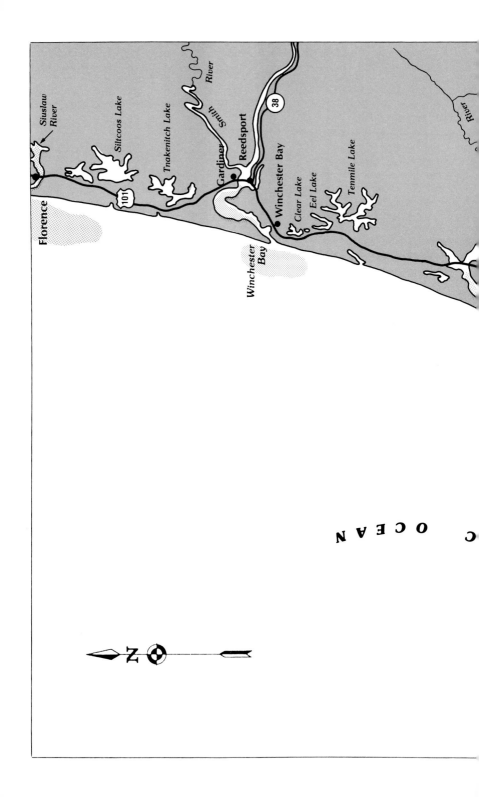

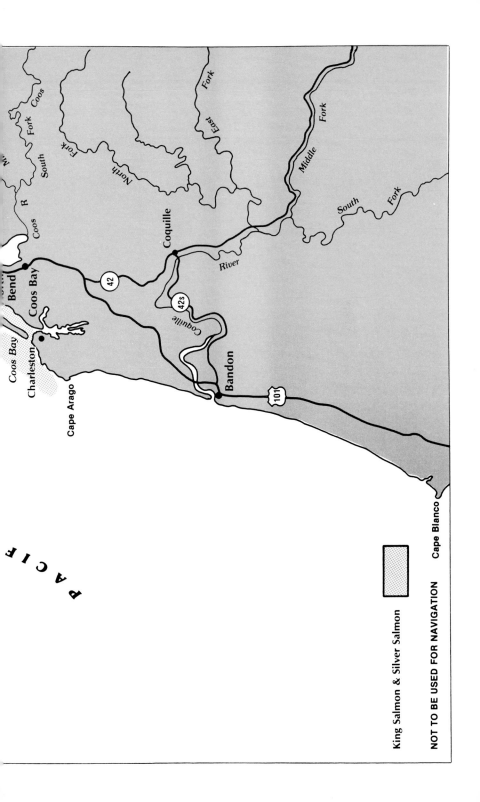

King Salmon & Silver Salmon

NOT TO BE USED FOR NAVIGATION

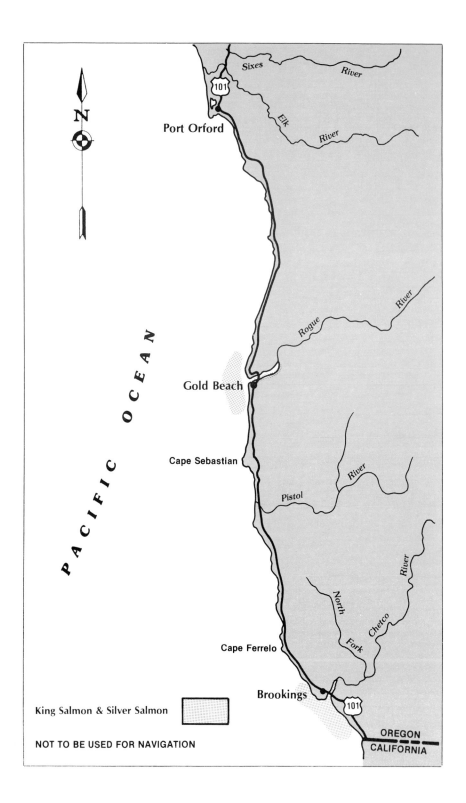

N

Sixes River

Elk River

101

Port Orford

P A C I F I C   O C E A N

Rogue River

Gold Beach

Cape Sebastian

Pistol River

Chetco River

North Fork

Cape Ferrelo

Brookings

101

OREGON
CALIFORNIA

King Salmon & Silver Salmon

NOT TO BE USED FOR NAVIGATION

On the ocean, anglers use planers here for both species, although downriggers have been gaining popularity. Chinook stick closer to the beach, and anglers will seek them from the mouth of the bay to just north of Nehalem, from about the 10-fathom line inward. For coho you fish farther out, starting at the 40- or 50-fathom line.

Inside the bay, a spreader and dropper is used for chinook — a sort of three-way swivel with one leg about 3 inches long, the other 1 1/2 inches long, with a weight on the short leg and a 6- foot leader on the other. Cut the leader in half and insert a bead chain swivel, then bait up with cut-plug herring.

Bay anglers here don't use the term mooch,' but that's what they do. They dangle their herring over the side of the boat, kicking their motors in and out of gear at very low speed. It's a crowded fishery, and your terminal tackle must be as nearly as possible directly under the boat, so sinkers of 4 to 6 ounces are common, and 12 ounces are not unusual.

It's important to fish deep. When you lower your rod, you should tap bottom.

The Tillamook bar can be tough, although it's generally good in the summer. It's usually no problem on a flood or a slack, and in summer sometimes can be crossed on the ebb, as long as it's not a big ebb.

About the last 100 yards of the north jetty on the seaward end are submerged, and conditions there can be dangerous. Avoid that part of the channel, and remember that the rest of the channel changes often from natural silting and scouring, so navigate cautiously. The bottom of the bay is mostly sand or mud. Rocks are a hazard only in one place, which is well marked.

Most ocean anglers launch at the Port of Garibaldi ramp or at the Old Mill Marina in Garibaldi. A couple of other ramps are farther from the mouth, and are popular for in-the-bay fishing.

Newport and Depoe Bay

As you move toward the central Oregon coast, more and more of the fishery centers on coho. Chinook are most prevalent at the northern and southern ends of the state, and interest in them declines from about Depoe Bay to Coos Bay. Most of the fishing here is done with a planer, and many anglers run a dodger or, less commonly, a flasher behind it, with herring. You can plug-cut your herring, or utilize strips, but whole herring is most common.

Some anglers will run a hoochie behind their planer, and many will stick a herring chunk − not a strip − on the trailing hook.

South of Tillamook Bay, the next real concentration of small-boat fishing takes place around Newport and Yaquina Bay. Heading seaward from the bay, you can start to fish around the whistle buoy, about 3 miles from the beach. Anglers are targeting coho here, although they'll occasionally pick up chinook.

The season usually opens around Memorial Day, and typically closes around Labor day, although fish will remain after that.

Tides don't make much difference here in when and how you fish. But a northwest wind, combined with an ebbing tide, can make for a sloppy bar.

Submerged rocks lie along the insides of both the north and south jetties, so you need to remain in the channel leaving and entering. Yaquina Reef lies parallel to the beach outside the north jetty, and always is dangerous, even in light winds. A large swell can cause a destructive breaker here with no warning, even in calm seas, and you never should fish near the reef. South Reef, which parallels the beach south of the south jetty, is an extension of Yaquina Reef, and is equally dangerous. When leaving the river, never turn north until you've passed Buoy No. 3, and never turn south until you have passed Buoy No. 1, to avoid the danger.

The Port of Newport operates one ramp, and it will accommodate three boats at a time if skippers know what they're doing.

A small-boat fleet also fishes out of Depoe Bay, about 13 miles to the north. It has a very narrow and hazardous channel, and it's important that you talk to knowledgeable local skippers before you attempt it. A boat clearing the entrance should proceed directly seaward until reaching the red bell buoy. Landward of that buoy to the north is North Reef. Seas can break over it from the northwest and southwest simultaneously, and you never should take a boat near it. South of the entrance is South Reef, also known as Flat Rock, and waves almost always are breaking here. Don't ever attempt to cross it when approaching the bay. Always run first to the bell buoy, then in from there.

Both North Reef and South Reef are unusually close to the channel, and in bad weather, breakers from North Reef may break right across the channel, making the harbor inaccessible.

Upwelling of the Pacific can bring cold water onto the beach anywhere along this coast, and that can result in fog at any time. Often the fog will burn off in the morning, but sometimes it might not lift for a week. Under these conditions, some anglers will follow a charterboat out. Others will navigate with Loran, and others will go out and in with just compass and dead-reckoning. But many anglers stay in their moorages then, not wanting to risk it.

An in-bay fishery also occurs near Newport for coho and chinook returning to a Weyerhaeuser aquaculture facility in Yaquina Bay. It takes place mainly in September, with anglers casting a wide variety of spinners from boats and from the beach. Find out what's working best when you are there, then just look for a crowd, and join it.

In September and October, in-bay fisheries for chinook also occur at Siletz and Alsea bays. Trolled bait fish is standard, although some anglers take jacks with eggs under bobbers. Both bays have launching facilities, but neither has an entrance jetty, and the mouths of both are very dangerous.

Florence and Reedsport

Farther down the coast beyond Alsea Bay lie Florence at the mouth of the Siuslaw River, and Reedsport near the mouth of the Umpqua River on Winchester Bay. Both areas offer excellent summer salmon angling.

The quality of the chinook fishing in both areas depends on the year. Coho fishing, however, generally always is good. The fish tend to arrive toward the end of June, and remain in these waters well into August. In fact, Winchester Bay has one of the most consistently productive coho catches throughout the season on the entire Oregon coast.

The top-notch action for silvers will begin winding down in both areas during the middle to latter part of August, and more chinook will begin to show in the catch then. The coho that anglers are catching here – as elsewhere on the Oregon coast – tend to be predominately Columbia River fish, which are working their way northward to the river mouth, so the fishing tends to last a little later in the season as you proceed north.

Anglers who fish off the coast here use a planer with flasher and hoochie for coho. Some use a downrigger. For chinook, they'll generally use a planer or a mooching weight, and will troll a whole bait fish.

The Siuslaw bar is a dangerous one with only a narrow channel extending past the jetties, and even a moderate swell may prevent small boats from crossing, especially on an ebb. Breakers may occur on the south side of the channel inside the jetties with even a small swell, and at the outer ends of both the north and south jetties.

At Winchester Bay near Reedsport, boaters should run along the inside of the south jetty leaving and entering. The area near the north jetty can be very dangerous, because it develops small breakers when a swell is running, and large breakers may come in from the outside. From the end of the north jetty to the black bell buoy, a little swell can result in breakers large enough to capsize a boat.

Late August through early September is when the in-bay fishery starts near Reedsport, and when the in-river fishery begins near Florence. They continue through October.

Florence has a fairly substantial fishery on wild chinook, but the biggest in-river fishery here for most of the season is for sea-run cutthroat trout. They're generally fished upstream from the town of Florence, 5 miles or more from the bar.

Launching at Florence is confined to the Port of Siuslaw ramp, a four-laner, which can be used without charge. The Reedsport area supports a substantial chinook fishery in the bay each fall, which typically starts about mid-August.

Near Reedsport, most saltwater anglers launch at the town of Winchester Bay, where county-operated Salmon Harbor Marina provides two one-lane ramps, both of which require a small fee. The marina offers 900 moorages with daily, weekly, monthly or annual rates.

Another one-laner, this one free, is available in Reedsport, on the Umpqua River, and another is located in Gardiner, a few miles north. These are used mostly by river fishermen and by clam diggers.

Coos Bay

Farther down the coast, around Coos Bay, large runs of coho start passing through about the middle to the end of June. They'll continue to come through at least a couple of weeks into August and then will begin to taper off.

Some boats, like this C-Dory, are loaded with usable fishing space.

The chinook fishery here has been growing in recent years, and can be good at times. Fish close to the beach for chinook. A private aquaculture facility here has been pumping fall chinook into the ocean for several years, and anglers here have an in-bay fishery that starts in April and runs until about the end of August, peaking in July.

The aquaculturists release both spring and fall chinook, and many anglers mooch near the bar for returning spring fish, which then mill in the bay all summer.

On the ocean, it's mostly a trolling scene. A typical angler uses a planer, about 3 feet of leader between it and a flasher, then 8 to 20 inches of leader tied to a hoochie with a herring chunk or strip. Some anglers use a whole herring instead of a hoochie, in which case they'll sometimes eliminate the flasher.

Anglers pick up chinook out of Coos Bay the entire season, generally inside the 25-fathom line, which is 2 to 3 miles from the beach. Coho usually are outside of 50 fathoms, although not always.

The Coos Bay Bar is one of the gentler on the coast. The channel is deep, and the water usually is fairly calm. Steep swells may build on the bar, but usually they won't break clear across. Sometimes, anglers even can cross on an ebbing tide, although not when the ocean is rough.

One word of warning, however: When departing the bay, be sure to clear Buoy No. 3 before turning north. The north jetty extends about 200 yards, submerged, past its visible terminus, and waves break in this area much of the time.

Launching facilities here are good. There's a four-lane ramp with floats in the hamlet of Charleston, near the harbor's mouth. Other ramps are available farther inland.

Port Orford

South of Coos Bay is Port Orford, which has no ramp. It has a sling, but very few sportsmen use it, for whatever reason. There is no real harbor here, no slips are available, and sport effort out of Port Orford is minimal.

Gold Beach and Brookings

Farther south on the coast is Gold Beach, where the fabled Rogue River spills into the Pacific, and south of there is Brookings and the mouth of the Chetco River. The two are a study in contrasts.

The Port of Brookings has the largest number of bar crossings in Oregon, after the Columbia River, but the bar is so kind you hardly can tell when you get to the ocean. In the Chetco River, inside the bar, are several modern ramps.

At Gold Beach, however, conditions can be treacherous. Many a boat has capsized in the surf here, and many an angler has drowned.

Some anglers fish only in the river at Gold Beach, inside the bar. Two public ramps are located here, one at the Port of Gold Beach, the other at Jot's Resort. Both are good ones. The in-river fishery occurs mostly in August and early September, and can attract a couple of hundred boats per day.

If you can get over the bar, ocean fishing often is excellent. Both coho and chinook are available from June into September. Chinook are headed for the Rogue, and the coho are bound for points farther north.

Anglers heading over the bar lean toward large boats with lots of horsepower. Tides are important, and wind is a factor, too. You must go in and out on the slack or the flood. Ebb tides can be lethal.

Inside the channel itself – between the jetties – gravel bars and shoals on the south side can create breakers to 6 feet when a heavy swell is running, and prevailing northwest summer winds can push you into them if you're not paying attention. At the outer ends of both jetties almost always are breakers, and when the sea is running from the west or the southwest, particularly, they can be very dangerous. The worst winds are from the south, which make the bar particularly rough. You can preview bar conditions, by the way, by driving out on the north jetty, from the community of Wedderburn.

Trolled frozen anchovies and frozen herring are popular bait in the ocean near Gold Beach, and generally are pulled behind a dodger or a flasher and fished with a Pink Lady or Deep Six. Twenty to 30 pulls of line will get you to the right depth. Occasionally, a sinker of 2 1/2 to 5 ounces is substituted for the planer.

Usually, the first three miles from the beach are where you find salmon, although the farther out you go the likelier you are to get into coho. Both species arrive about the same time, but from about the middle of August on, it's primarily chinook. They gather off the river mouth, where they strike readily at baits or lures.

The fish here are big. Expect chinook to run 12 to 30 pounds, with a few to 40, and the average 22 to 27 pounds. Silvers run 8 to 14 pounds.

Anglers tend to target chinook off Brookings, too, although harvests of both species are excellent. The Rogue has tremendous runs of chinook, and some of its stocks are south-turning, so anglers at Brookings are the beneficiaries. Most of the coho are headed for more northerly Oregon coastal streams and, of course, for the Columbia River.

Fishing starts usually in late May or early June off the southern Oregon coast, and generally runs through September. Sometimes, regulations provide for some extended sport seasons to continue through October off the Chetco and off the Elk River, which is farther north near Cape Blanco, usually in a narrow coastal strip.

Like the Rogue, the Chetco offers fishing inside the bar, mainly in the fall. Anglers take some huge fish here then, with the ten largest each fall often in the 50- to 60-pound range. September and October are peak in-river months here, a little later than in the Rogue. Good fishing continues until the first heavy fall rains, when the fish move upriver.

* * *

Chapter Fifteen

California Coast

YOU'D THINK THAT AS AN ANGLER MOVED south along the Pacific coast, out of the Pacific Northwest and into California, the fishing would decline. But that's not the case at all.

If anything, it gets better. The rugged California coastline from Crescent City near the Oregon border, all the way to Monterey Bay between San Francisco and Los Angeles, offers nearly unlimited opportunity for small-boat salmon angling.

Far and away, the vast majority of small-boat fishing, called "skiff fishing" in California, takes place out of Crescent City and Eureka. But nearly anyplace along the coast from the northern border to Monterey an angler can find good opportunity at the right time of year to bring some salmon to the net. Some places are better than others, of course, and some offer easier fishing opportunity.

California fishing is a lot like that in Oregon in one important respect. California anglers tend not to mooch, for whatever reason, although the technique has been finding favor lately in Monterey Bay. In general, though it's pretty much a trolling show in California both for coho and chinook.

Crescent City

This is the hub of the action for big chinook salmon in California, and anglers stream in from all over when the bite gets hot. Whopper kings that take two arms to lift are pulled into skiffs here using the same basic strategies that work well in Oregon and Washington.

Many anglers use a planer ahead of a flasher and a fresh or frozen anchovy or herring. A few use a hoochie behind the flasher, with a nice baitfish strip on the trailing hook.

The middle of July to the middle of August usually produces the best fishing for chinook, and it's well worth the time to be here then, because many of these fish run to 40 pounds and more. Coho fill the waters between the first of August and the first of September.

The single three-lane launching ramp in Crescent City is adequate, but can be a fairly busy place on a summer morning.

Crescent City has a good harbor, and one of the nicest things about it is that there is no bar, so conditions are good for small boats. Often, you can be into salmon as little as 300 yards off the jetty, and 6 or 8 miles is about as far as you ever should have to run – not out into the ocean, but south and a little west from the harbor mouth. Anglers often troll in as little as 60 feet of water, and it's hardly ever necessary to go beyond the 40-fathom mark. Fog can be a problem here, as it can anywhere along the coast. Sometimes when it's foggy you might see 60 boats going around and around Buoy 2, about a mile outside the harbor, and a lot of them might be catching fish.

Eureka

It's a different story at Eureka. Tides control the fishing here, because a formidable bar lies at the mouth of Humboldt Bay. That means you can fish only on the flood, because the ebb usually creates a dangerous crossing situation. Even on a flood you have to watch the weather, because it can get rough here in a hurry, and fog can come down without warning.

Salmon are in this area spring through fall, so finding them is no problem within the seasons set by the Pacific Fishery Management Council. By the first of June the ocean usually settles down enough to become fishable, and June through July is when the bulk of the fishing takes place. It's important to keep in mind that you've got only a six- or seven-hour fishing day, however. You can cross the bar at low slack going out, but you'd better be back by high slack, or you're probably going to have a long wait at sea for the bar to settle down.

The author with two nice chinook — the kind you can catch regularly by utilizing the principles in this book.

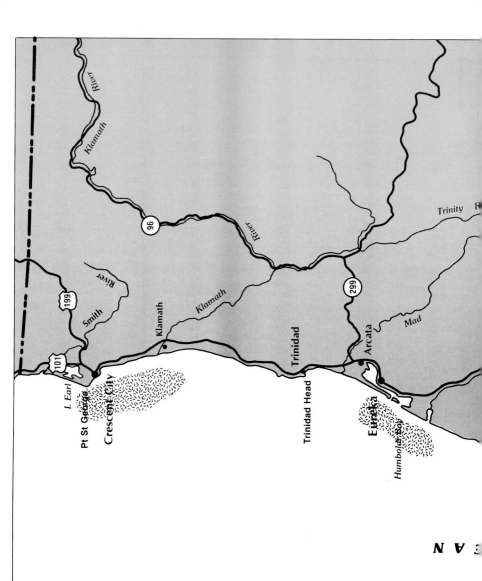

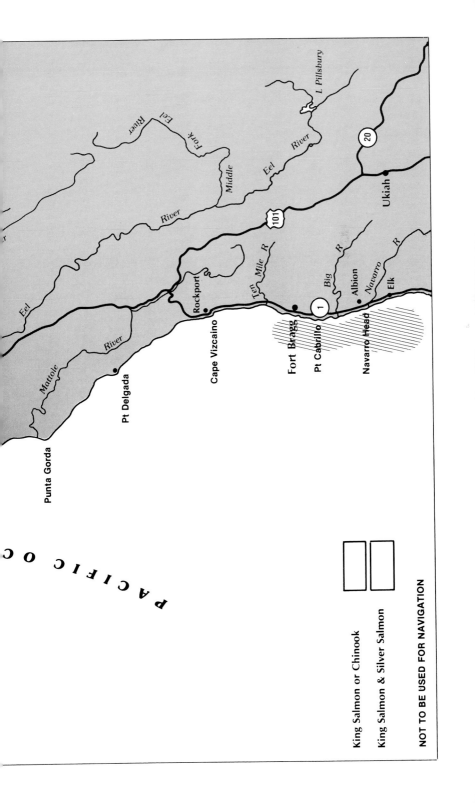

King Salmon or Chinook

King Salmon & Silver Salmon

NOT TO BE USED FOR NAVIGATION

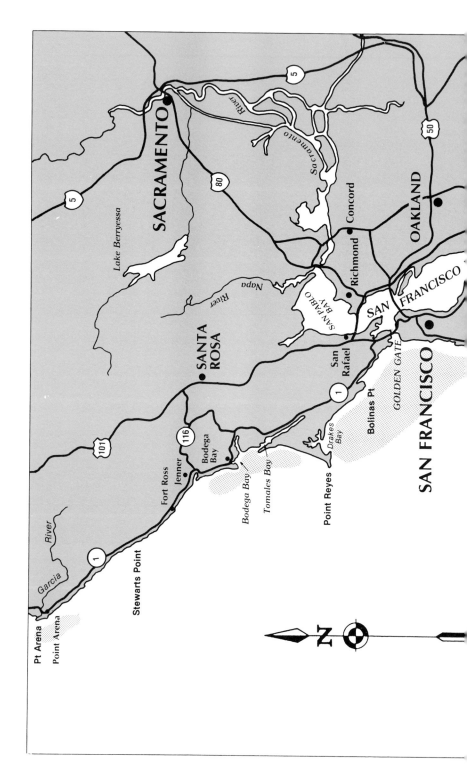

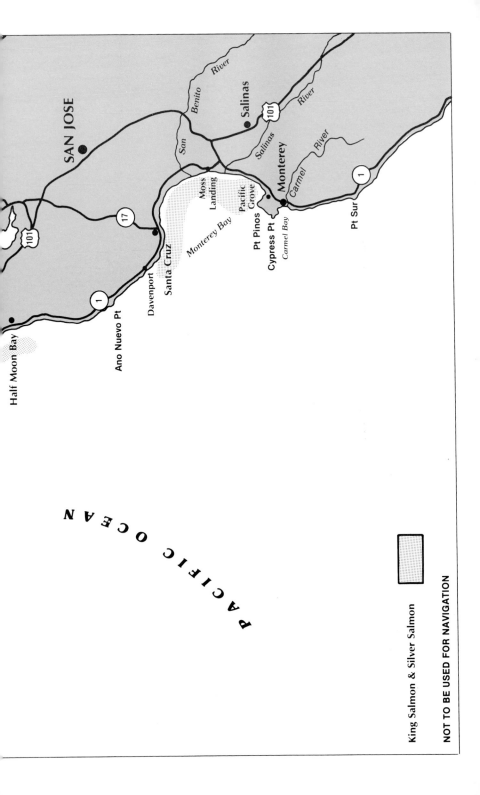

SAN JOSE

Half Moon Bay

Ano Nuevo Pt

Davenport

Santa Cruz

Monterey Bay

Moss Landing

Pacific Grove

Pt Pinos

Cypress Pt

Carmel Bay

Monterey

Pt Sur

Salinas

San Benito River

San

Salinas River

Carmel River

101

17

1

1

101

PACIFIC OCEAN

King Salmon & Silver Salmon

NOT TO BE USED FOR NAVIGATION

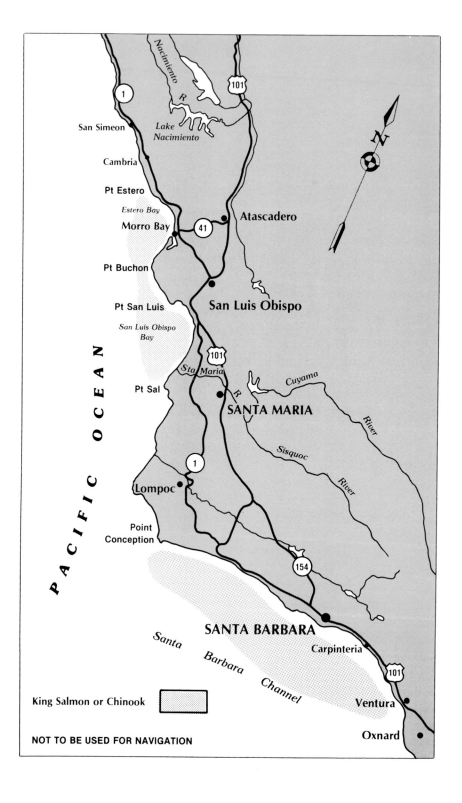

NOT TO BE USED FOR NAVIGATION

As at Crescent City, anchovies are the preferred bait here, fished on a two-hook rig, and generally pulled whole behind a planer and a flasher. The same gear is used for both coho and chinook. The catch is about half and half, with Eureka pretty much the southern end of the main Pacific coho fishery.

A lot of anglers use Dipsy Diver planers here, which can be set to take a line to the left or to the right of the boat as well as down. That permits the anglers to run more lines than they can with divers that fish directly off the stern.

Both coho and chinook usually are available right out front, between imaginary points about a mile north and a mile south of the harbor. The bulk of the fishing takes place within a couple of miles of the beach, much of it around the whistler buoy, a mile from the harbor entrance, although anglers sometimes run 3 or 4 miles out to find the schools.

Lots of trailerable boats fish out of Eureka, and launching is adequate. Humboldt Bay has several public ramps, and several private ones.

The official season often runs into September here, but very little fishing occurs after the first of August in a typical year. Most of the coho are moving on by then toward their natal streams in Oregon, and chinook are moving into the Klamath, the Smith, the Eel, the Mad and other north coast rivers and streams. The fishery peaks about the end of June and the first part of July, for both species.

Cape Mendocino which juts into the Pacific south of Eureka divides federal salmon-management areas, and south of the cape the rules are more liberal. The season generally runs from mid-February to mid-November. Most of the sport catch from here all the way to the southern limits of the fishery, near Santa Barbara, is Sacramento River stock. And that means chinook. Fewer and fewer coho show in the catch as you go south, because very few are produced in the Sacramento system. A few return to some small streams in the drainage, and a couple of private hatcheries rear coho there in ocean-ranching enterprises. But most of the few that are caught are just passing through on their way to Oregon, or to a handful of streams near California's northern end.

Fort Bragg to Tomales Bay

Several ramps are available at Fort Bragg between Eureka and San Francisco. Another is at Albion, about 18 miles south of Fort Bragg, and a hoist-type launch is located at Point Arena, about 30 miles south of Albion.

Between Point Arena and Bodega Bay there's virtually no place to launch, but Spud Point Marina at Bodega has facilities, and so does Lawson's Landing in Tomales Bay, just south of Bodega.

San Francisco

South of Point Reyes, expect to see a lot of San Francisco-based partyboats. They venture north along the Marin County coast, south as far as Half Moon Bay, and seaward about 20 miles to the Farallon Islands, due west of the Golden Gate. The whole area is known as the Gulf of the Farallons, and is very productive, because anglers here don't have to wait for migratory fish. They target 2-year-old resident fish that feed here all year long, and pick up significant numbers of migrants as well.

A vigorous small-boat fishery operates out of San Francisco Bay, but it has its drawbacks. It's a fairly long run to the ocean from launching areas inside, through heavy marine traffic, unpredictable winds and dangerous currents. Fog can come down in an instant, and can be especially dangerous in an area as heavily traveled as this. Anglers can launch at Half Moon Bay, but heavy highway tourist traffic there, especially on weekends, can make for an aggravating day.

Monterey to Morro Bay

From San Francisco it's a couple of hours by car to Monterey Bay, the next-closest launching area. There, anglers fish primarily in the bay itself, which tends to be on-again, off-again, because it holds no resident salmon. Sacramento chinook are the target here, and they're just passing through. Expect the fishery to be hot for a while, then slow for a week or so. This tends to be an early fishery, with the best action in April and May.

The Santa Cruz Yacht Harbor has good launching facilities on the northern end of the bay. The next available launch is at Moss Landing, between Santa Cruz and Monterey, and facilities also are located in Monterey itself, which has a couple of ramps.

The coast is virtually empty of launch facilities from Monterey to Morro Bay, near the southern end of the salmon's range, and where sport catches tend to be sparse. Although the season generally opens in February here, fish usually don't show up in any numbers until a couple of months later, when anglers take 3- and 4-year-old chinook bound for the Sacramento. Often, the Morro Bay fishery lasts only a week or two, but some years, depending on currents and water temperatures, salmon will remain in the area several weeks.

In good years, partyboats from Ventura will take salmon in the Santa Barbara Channel. But don't count on finding salmon in catchable numbers south of Morro Bay – it's always a gamble whether they'll migrate close enough for skiff fishermen to go after them.

* * *

Chapter Sixteen

Crossing the Bar

WHETHER IT'S PRODUCTIVITY OR NATURAL beauty, there's hardly a better place in the world for an angler than the spectacular Northwest coast.

But the lovely waters extract their price. They can be treacherous, and small-boat anglers need to realize it and respect the conditions that can get them into trouble.

Fog and wind and rough seas can be hazards any time. But the most dangerous thing a small-boat angler faces here may be crossing the bars from the bays to the sea. To do it, you've got to understand what a bar is, how it works, and what its characteristics are at every location.

A bar is a shallow area at the mouth of a river or bay where incoming ocean swells may turn into breaking waves. Bars are most dangerous on an ebb tide, when water from the bay is flowing seaward. Particularly when the ebb is supplemented by a river current, the outward flow of water can be tremendous, and when it collides with the incoming surf, huge waves can stack up.

Talk to other anglers – experienced ones – where you

plan to fish, and follow their example. If bar conditions are rough, stay inside until they improve. If you're fishing outside, pay attention to the stage of the tide, and get back inside again before the ebb begins.

Remember, all things being equal, it's easier to get out over a rough bar than it is to get in. Going out, you're headed into the seas, and you have better control of your boat. Coming in, the seas are astern, reducing your maneuverability. Keep in mind also that it's easier to judge a bar from the landward side, where you can more easily see any breakers. From seaward, breakers may not be visible, and the bar may look calmer than it is.

If you get into trouble coming in, try to keep the incoming seas squarely astern. Keep one hand on the throttle, and try to ride the back of a swell, keeping clear of the following wave. Do not allow your boat to turn sideways to the seas. That's called broaching, and it can result in capsizing.

* * *

Salmon Identification

Five species of native salmon are found on the Pacific coast of North America. They are:

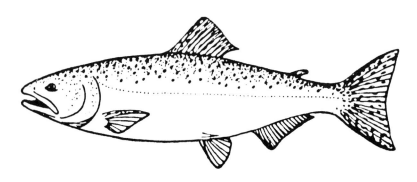

Chinook *(Oncorhynchus tshawytscha)* – Also known as king, spring salmon, tyee (in Canada), blackmouth (in immature form). The largest of the Pacific salmon, and the most sought after by sport fishermen, mature specimens commonly exceed 20 pounds, and often will weigh in the 30s and 40s. Larger individuals are not as common, but are not unusual. The all-tackle world record of 97 pounds, 4 ounces was taken in 1985 in Alaska's Kenai River. In the 1950s, a chinook weighing 102 pounds was gaffed in Washington's Elwha River. Chinook can be persistent fighters, and large ones can strip a reel. Recognizable by a heavily spotted back, spots on both lobes of the tail, and a black gumline at the base of its teeth on its lower jaw. The tip of its lower jaw is pointed.

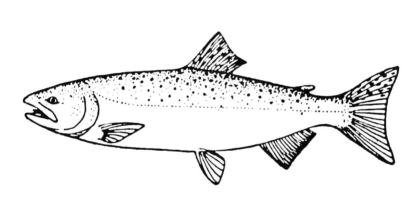

Coho *(Oncorhynchus kisutch)* — Also known as silver, matures at 2 or 3 years, and may exceed 30 pounds. A coho weighing in the low to middle teens is considered large, however. More lightly spotted than a chinook, its tail has spots only on the upper lobe. The lower gumline is gray at the base of the teeth, and the lower jaw is rounded at the tip. Spectacular fighters, they love to leap out of the water when hooked.

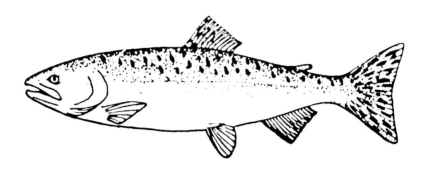

Pink *(Oncorhynchus gorbuscha)* – Also known as humpback or humpy, matures at 2 years and may weigh into the middle teens, although usually smaller. Hard fighters. Particularly good for smoking. Heavily spotted on back and tail, can be identified by unusually small scales. Run only in odd-numbered years in Washington.

◆━━━━━━━━━━━━━━━━━━━━━━◆

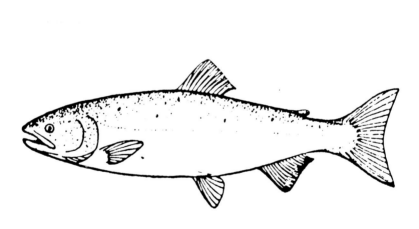

Chum *(Oncorhynchus keta)* – Also known as dog salmon because of toothy lower jaw at maturity, lives 3 to 5 years, and may weigh as much as 30 pounds. Mature specimens commonly reach the high teens and low 20s. Do not take bait or lures readily, but when they do are tenacious fighters, possibly tougher pound-for-pound than any other Pacific salmon. Mature specimens may be recognized by vertical shading on sides. Also, for their size, chums are unusually small in circumference at the spot just ahead of the lobes of the tail.

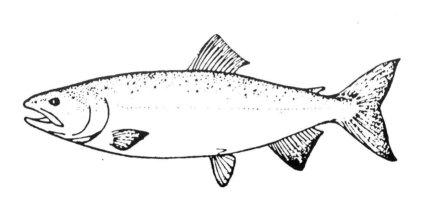

Sockeye *(Oncorhynchus nerka)* – Also known as red salmon, are rarely taken on sport gear in saltwater in the United States. However, a popular sport fishery is developing off the west coast of Vancouver Island, where anglers take them on small red lures, trolled deep and slow. A sport fishery sometimes takes place in Lake Washington, at Seattle, where anglers troll flatfish or bare, colored hooks, also slow and deep. Only fair fighters, they can grow to about 15 pounds, but mature specimens more commonly run 6 to 10 pounds. They can be recognized by their prominent eyes.

* * *

How to Rig Herring

To rig plug-cut herring, start with bright, unmarked bait; fresh if possible. Slice off head, cutting on angle from front to back as shown, and also on an angle from top to bottom by tilting back of blade to right. This puts a beveled edge on bait to help make it spin. Practice will teach you at how sharp an angle the bevel should be.

Remove entrails with head. They must be removed to obtain proper action from bait.

Insert trailing hook of two-hook mooching rig into body cavity and out through short side of beveled bait. Pull entire hook out through the hole.

Insert leading hook of two-hook mooching rig into body cavity and out near spine.

Plug-cut herring is ready to fish. You may let trailing hook dangle, or you may anchor it in bait near the tail, with the point exposed. Always test bait for proper action by pulling it alongside boat before fishing. Bait should spin erratically, imitating injured herring.

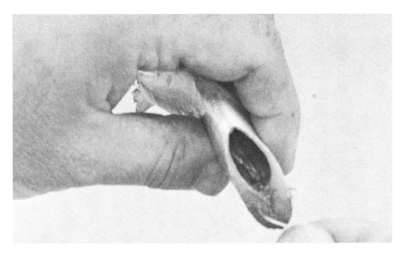

Alternate method, insert trailing hook through fleshy portion of herring above body cavity, exiting on side of herring.

Pull trailing hook all the way through hole, and insert leading hook into same hole.

Pull leading hook all the way through hole, then insert it just behind hole and anchor it high in side of herring near spine, with tip exposed.

Tighten leading hook by pulling on leader above it, drawing eye of hook back into original hole through which both trailing hook and leading hook were inserted.

Bait is ready to fish. Always test it in water before fishing.

Simplest of many ways to rig a whole herring, and a very effective one, is to insert leading hook through head between herring's eye and mouth, from left to right.

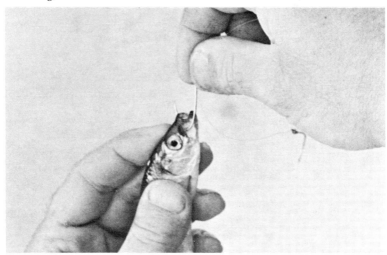

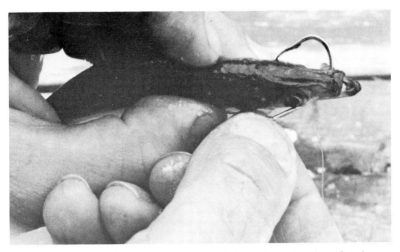

Without pulling hook all the way through hole, turn shank and re-insert point into head behind herring's eye. Push point all the way through head, so it emerges on same side of head as hook's eye. Simply let trailing hook dangle.

Ready to fish. Always test by pulling alongside boat before fishing.

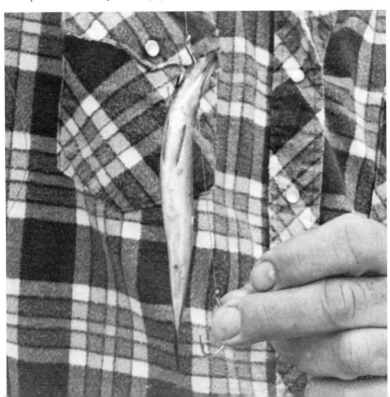

Salmon Filleting

To fillet a salmon properly, you need a hard cutting surface and a good-quality, flexible fillet knife. Give the knife a few strokes on the stone each time you use it. It must by sharp to do the job well.

Scale your salmon by directing a hard stream of water from a garden hose along the fish from tail to head, opposite the direction in which the scales lie. Now slice through the neck to the spine, just behind the gill cover.

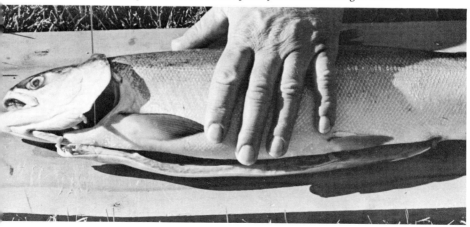

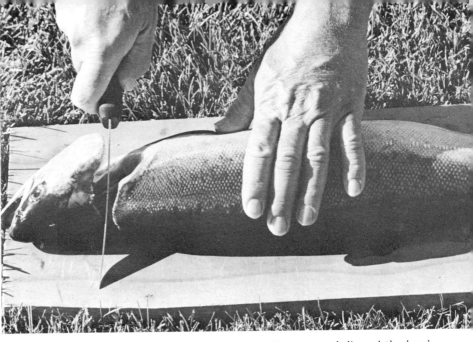

Turn the fish over and complete the cut. Remove and discard the head. (Some people retain heads and backbones for soup stock or crab bait. They may be frozen until needed.)

Lay knife against top side of spine, blade parallel with ground, and begin slicing toward tail. Keep the blade flat, and cut through ribs as you proceed.

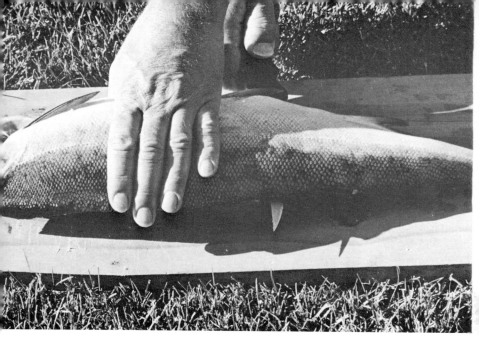

Continue slicing all the way to tail, keeping blade flat atop spine the entire distance.

Top side of fish will come away from the rest of the carcass at the tail.

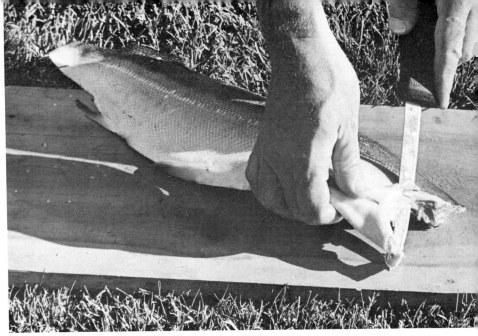

Trim off the curved cleithrum bone and the pectoral fin that is attached.

Lay piece skin-side down and, starting near center line, trim away ribs in one piece, holding knife blade flat and slicing carefully through meat just below ribs. Discard ribs.

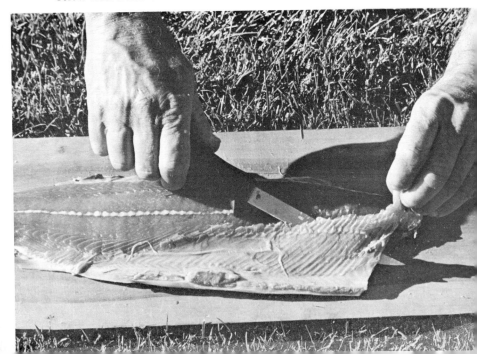

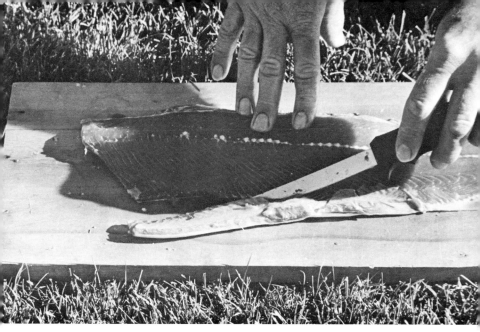

Remove and discard fatty belly strip.

Turn other half of fish flesh-side down and repeat process, slicing carefully along top of spine with flat blade to remove meaty portion from spine. Repeat steps 7, 8, and 9.

Slice each side into serving-size portions.

The finished product. Tail sections are bone-free. One line of rib-size bones remains in each of the other pieces, but bones are large and easy to avoid when eating.

Index